THE NARROW WAY

PAUL CARTER

THE NARROW WAY

© 2012 Paul Carter

Unless otherwise indicated, all Scripture quotations marked NRSV are taken from The Holy Bible: New Revised Standard Version/Division of Christian Education of the National Council of Churches of Christ in the United States of America. Nashville: Thomas Nelson Publishers. Copyright © 1989. Used by permission. All rights reserved. Scripture quotations marked ESV are from The Holy Bible, English Standard Version® (ESV®), copyright © 2001 by Crossway, a publishing ministry of Good News Publishers. Used by permission. All rights reserved. Scripture quotations marked NKJV are taken from the New King James Version®. Copyright © 1982 by Thomas Nelson, Inc. Used by permission. All rights reserved. Scripture quotations marked KJV are taken from the Holy Bible, King James Version, which is in the public domain.

ISBN: 978-1-77069-530-6

Printed in Canada

Word Alive Press
131 Cordite Road, Winnipeg, MB R3W 1S1
www.wordalivepress.ca

Library and Archives Canada Cataloguing in Publication

Carter, Paul, 1974-
    The narrow way / Paul Carter.
ISBN 978-1-77069-530-6
    1. Christian life. 2. Bible--Theology. I. Title.
BV4501.3.C379 2012   248.4   C2012-901755-8

To Shauna Lee,

who lives out the belief that it takes two people to live one great life. Your share in this is larger than mine.

Contents

Dedication	iii
Acknowledgements	vii
Introduction	1
Prologue	
Setting Out and Sitting Down at the Feet of the Master	9
Chapter One	
Blessed Are the Poor in Spirit, for Theirs is Kingdom of Heaven	13
Chapter Two	
Blessed Are Those Who Mourn, for They Will be Comforted	29
Chapter Three	
Blessed Are the Meek, for They Will Inherit the Earth	46
Chapter Four	
Blessed Are Those Who Hunger and Thirst for Righteousness, for They Shall Be Filled	63
Chapter Five	
Blessed Are the Merciful, for They Shall Obtain Mercy	83
Chapter Six	
Blessed Are the Pure in Heart, for They Shall See God	104
Chapter Seven	
Blessed Are the Peacemakers, for They Shall Be Called Sons of God	123
Chapter Eight	
Blessed Are Those Who Are Persecuted for Righteousness' Sake, for Theirs Is the Kingdom of Heaven	156
Chapter Nine	
The Witnesss of the Fully Converted Church—Salt and Light	183
Epilogue	201

Acknowledgements

The hardest part about writing a book is fitting all the people who are owed thanks and tribute into one paragraph. I apologize in advance to those who deserve to be mentioned and who aren't. I would first like to thank all of the people from King Bible Church, the church I grew up in. I'm not sure if you even remember me but you taught me to fear God, love his Son, read his Word and live among his people. I owe you my life and can never repay that debt. Thank you. It is so common today for people my age to bear a grudge against "the church". I don't know who they are talking about. You were so good to me and so kind and so healthy and so right about so many things. Blessings be upon you. To my wife and children I also want to express deep love and appreciation. Thank you for sharing me and for cheering me on. I have never had to choose between my God and my family and you make putting God first a pain free decision. I really appreciate that. I also want to thank my wife's parents who loaned me their smoky back woods cabin. I can't imagine a better place to write a book. I want to write more books just so that I can chop wood, use your chemical toilet and sleep under that crazy electric blanket. I'm not sure if that is a healthy motivation, but I admit it freely. I would also like to thank my church. Thank you for being an overflow church. Thank you for being healthy but not insular. Thank you for robbing any motivation I may ever have had to gripe about "the church" or "religious people". You are living out faith in a wonderfully healthy way and I wish I could share you with other people in other places. Thank you for sharing me with them and letting me do the other things God has called me to do. It is always easy to come back home and be with you. Thank you!

Lastly, and most importantly I want to thank God. How I love your Word! How I marvel at your holiness, your goodness and your mercy! I am so thankful for my salvation and so consumed by the beauty of the cross. O for a thousand tongues to sing and a thousand lives to lie down in your service! You are God and you are good and I am at peace. To God alone be the glory. Even so come Lord Jesus.

Introduction

There was a season in the life of my church when the anointing of the Holy Spirit was very powerfully upon us for evangelism. People were getting saved in the strangest ways. It wasn't about me or the power of our presentation; there was just something of the purpose of God in it. It was as though the aroma of life was hovering over our church and people were drawing near to breathe it in. One man even came to Christ in our offices because God had tugged on his ear as he drove by and told him to come inside.

It was a wonderful season. We had hundreds of people come to Christ… and then it stopped. People are still coming to Christ, one or two or five or six every month, but nothing like the bunches and clumps from that season. That season was almost four years ago now and it has been very interesting to watch the people who were pulled, drawn, and summoned to the Gospel and observe their progress. It was this season and those people who inspired us to create the resource that became the book *Mile 1*.

Mile 1 was written because we had a ton of people respond to the Gospel who had no idea what it was like to follow Jesus and no concept of how saved people lived. *Mile 1* was what the title suggested—it was Christianity 101, or rather "the first mile of the narrow way." It focused on the sixteen major changes that a converted person would have to process in order to effectively follow Jesus. I've described it many times as being rather like the onramp to the highway. In a sense, it is the highway, but in another sense it is just how you get on the highway.

Mile 1 was well-used. We initially created it just to help our own new people get up to speed. We had no idea that God would use it to help Christians all over the world begin making the basic changes that must follow the decision to repent and follow Jesus.

Martin Luther famously began his world-shaking thesis by suggesting that the entire Christian journey is a daily commitment to repentance. You wake up every morning and say: "My instincts and my preferences point me in such and such a direction, and yet I know that the end of such things is death. I know that all of my desires, all of my opinions, and all of my inclinations are only evil all the time. My sense of direction is entirely clouded by my ignorance, my arrogance, and my selfishness. I simply cannot be trusted to make decisions today that will glorify God and bless other people. Therefore, I will die to them all. I will deny myself, take up my cross, and follow Jesus. I will think with his thoughts, speak with his words, and walk in his steps. I will be penitent today. I will be a Christian, by God's grace."

I think Luther had it right, really right, and I think we may need another Reformation that starts with that idea. Christianity has become far too associated with "a decision" and "a sincere belief"—or even worse, "a sinner's prayer." We've turned faith into a transaction based on momentary sentiment and sincerity. The transaction looks like this: "I give you one moment of tearful prayer and sincere thanksgiving and you give me eternal life, and also a little prosperity, if you don't mind." There is very little thought as to what comes next. There is very little thought as to whether that is even a

Introduction

valid starting point. Our Gospel has been changed by our culture whereas once our culture was changed by our Gospel.

We are a culture dominated by transactions. We buy things. In the aftermath of 9/11, it was surreal to hear President Bush tell the American people what they should do to help the country in her hour of need: go shopping. The American economy is fuelled by customer transactions. If we don't buy plastic nonsense from China, our whole world will collapse. It's small wonder that we have turned the Gospel into a transaction. It's small wonder, but it's also of tremendous concern. The Gospel is not that kind of transaction. We do not purchase our salvation with a little prayer. Salvation is not a ticket that we sew into our underwear as insurance against Armageddon. It's none of those things.

It's so rare to hear people in the Bible speak about salvation as something they possess. Rather, with holy reverence and humble hesitation, they always speak of it in a present continuous sense, as something walked in, as something hoped for, as something perpetually received. Listen to how the Apostle Paul talked about salvation:

> But since we belong to the day, let us be sober, having put on the breastplate of faith and love, and for a helmet the hope of salvation. For God has not destined us for wrath, but to obtain salvation through our Lord Jesus Christ, who died for us so that whether we are awake or asleep we might live with him. Therefore encourage one another and build one another up, just as you are doing. (1 Thessalonians 5:8–11, ESV)

Paul talks about salvation as something God destined us to receive, something that is a certain hope, held out in front of us so we may walk forward in it as a tribe and by his grace. That doesn't sound like a ticket sewn into my underwear. Neither does it sound that way in Philippians 2:

> Therefore, my beloved, as you have always obeyed, so now, not only as in my presence but much more in my absence, work out your own salvation with fear and trembling, for it is God who works in you, both to will and to work for his good pleasure. (Philippians 2:12–13, ESV)

Work out your salvation. God is at work in you. That sounds like more than a ticket and more than a transaction; it sounds like a walk. It sounds a little thicker than the way we normally talk about salvation.

I wrote *Mile 1* because I wanted our people to understand that after the decision there is a walk. After the prayer, there is a life of penitence. After the narrow gate, there is a narrow way. I wanted our people to have a thicker understanding of conversion. I wanted them to understand that conversion is not the same as clarity, not the same as confession, and not the same as conviction. Conversion includes all of those ideas, but it's more. It's a whole new way of living. A different way. A narrow way. A Jesus way. I wrote *Mile 1* to get people moving, but this book shows where I wanted them to land.

Something else happened during that blessed season in our church. It wasn't just that people were drawn from strange places to respond to the Gospel, it was also that strange people were drawn to respond to the Gospel. What was strangest of all was how many of them had been long-time members of our church. I figure that about a third of the people who got saved over that two-year season were either members or long-time adherents of either our church or some other evangelical church in town.

This actually caused some serious concern and embarrassment among a few of our elders. I remember one dear brother saying with concern, "I was a little bit horrified to see brother so-and-so respond to the Gospel on Sunday given that I interviewed him for membership years ago and recommended him without reservation!" What do you do when a man who has been a member of your church for almost ten years becomes a Christian? I think you have to take stock of how well you have been teaching about conversion.

Dr. Martyn Lloyd Jones, in his incredibly useful book *Preaching and Preachers*,[1] said that one of the biggest mistakes a pastor can make is assuming that his members are truly converted. I no longer assume that. I did for a long time. Now I'm committed to working out salvation with my people. I'm committed to helping them—and, indeed, helping me—understand that repentance isn't something you did once, a long time ago, that night you felt sentimental at the campfire. Repentance is something you do every day if you are truly a converted person.

Every day I have to wake up and say, "Not my way, but your way." Obviously a huge part of that commitment is the determination to actually know the Jesus way. If you are going to be converted—that is, if you are going to *stop* living your way, *stop* living the world's way—then you have to be clear as to which new way you will be living, by God's grace. You have to live some way. So which way?

Happily, we are not left to wonder what the fully converted life looks like. Jesus told us. He gave us the beatitudes in his famous Sermon on the Mount. The beatitudes are not a description of how to get saved, but rather a description of the fully converted life. They are what we must go back to, every day, as the outline of the

---

[1] Jones, Dr. Martyn Lloyd. *Preaching and Preachers* (Grand Rapids, MI: Zondervan, 2011).

Jesus way. My flesh tells me to be my own God; the beatitudes tell me to be poor in spirit. My flesh tells me to seek revenge; the beatitudes tell me to be merciful. This is not a natural way. It is a narrow way and only the born again can walk it.

This book is a helpful follow-up for those who have been set to motion in their faith by studying *Mile 1*, but it is also meant to stand alone. It's not specifically for new believers. Rather, it's for anyone who wants to continue to work out their salvation. The format is designed to facilitate individual or small group study and it can be profitably used either way. There are small group discussion tasks at the end of each chapter and also a section for self-evaluation. All readers, whether reading as an individual or as part of a small group, should make careful use of this section. Lloyd Jones would remind me as an author not to assume that any of my readers are truly converted. He would remind you to be wary of being too sure yourself. He might quote the Apostle Paul, who said:

> Therefore let anyone who thinks that he stands take heed lest he fall. (1 Corinthians 10:12, ESV)

Use the self-evaluation section to honestly hold up your life against the pattern of the beatitudes. Evangelical scholars and Bible teachers generally agree that this is a description of what every truly saved person looks like. If you don't look at all this way, you must honestly conclude that you are not truly converted. That is a wonderful discovery! To miss that discovery would be an unspeakable horror. Now, I don't mean to say that every believer will be equally strong in all areas of comparison; we are all in different stages of sanctification, but all believers should show growth in the same direction if they are truly converted.

The observance of stage-appropriate growth is an accepted proof of life in the medical field, and this should serve as an analogy for the spiritual realm. My wife and I have five children, so I am well-acquainted with the various stage examinations that accompany a pregnancy. At a certain number of weeks, the doctor expects to hear a heartbeat. At another stage, she expects to be able to take a picture. At another stage, the sex of the child should be visible. These appropriate markers do not make the baby alive; rather, they simply prove and assure that the baby is alive. So it is with the beatitudes. They do not make you saved—only the sovereign electing grace of God can do that. But if a mother went to an appointment where a heartbeat was expected and none was found, she would be anxious. If she next went to an appointment and there was no weight gain, no heartbeat, and no hormones in the blood screen, she would panic and demand a full evaluation. Why is it that we approach eternal life with so much less attention and so much more blind assurance? Use the self-evaluation. Have the poverty of spirit to accept the results as a valid testimony to your spiritual life. If there was sovereign conception, there will be signs of life. How do I know this? Because the Bible says:

> I am sure of this, that he who began a good work in you will bring it to completion at the day of Jesus Christ. (Philippians 1:6, ESV)

God always finishes what he starts. Every conception ends in the birth of eternal life, but there is a lot of living along the way. This is a description of that way.

> "Come, follow me…"
> —Jesus

Prologue

Setting Out and Sitting Down at the Feet of the Master

It will be obvious to most readers already that the basic structure and content of this book is taken from the Sermon on the Mount. Viewed by most Christian theologians as the core of Jesus' teaching content and treasured by most believers as among the sweetest words in Scripture, the Sermon presents a thorough and powerful description of fully converted Christian living.

When Dr. Martyn Lloyd Jones prefaced his massive volume entitled *Studies in the Sermon on the Mount*,[2] he said that he had preached thirty Sundays in a row on the Sermon because of the massive superficiality of Christians in his day. He felt so strongly about the corrective benefit of the Sermon on the Mount that he expanded and organised his sermons into a nearly six-hundred-page book that is now widely recognised as an evangelical classic.

---

2   Jones, Dr. Martyn Lloyd. *Studies in the Sermon on the Mount* (Grand Rapids, MI: Eerdmans, 1959–1960).

The Sermon on the Mount is the bread of life. It is the Word of God and we need to draw near unto it again.

When you listen to the Sermon on the Mount, you must hear it as a description of what the kingdom is. The kingdom is a place without sin. It is a place that aligns perfectly with the will of God. It is a place where people look a lot like God because they are children of their father in heaven. Yet it exists at present within a dying place, and in that sense it is like salt or light. The kingdom is in this world, but it is not like this world; in the end, it will become this world.

We must not speak of it as an unachievable ideal as though to say, "No one could actually live that way." The whole point of the Gospel is that by God's grace, empowered by God's Spirit, we will indeed live that way—increasingly *now* and entirely *then*. Our righteousness will, in fact, far surpass that of the Pharisees. That's not to say that Christians will never sin in this life; it's to say that there is no sin in the kingdom of God. If a teacher should say to his Grade Five class, "We do not chew gum in my classroom," it would be a foolish boy indeed who raised his hand to say, "But teacher, I am in fact chewing gum." That is to miss the point. We do not chew gum in here; that is the point.[3] When you hear the Sermon on the Mount, you should hear Jesus saying, "This is the kingdom way. This is the kingdom witness. This is the kingdom walk." Yes, there are weeds. Yes, there is mixture. But there is *kingdom,* and the kingdom will grow and endure… and in the end there will be only kingdom, thanks be to God.

As we walk through this teaching, you should see what the kingdom of heaven is. If you are indeed fully converted and "born from above," then the kingdom should be increasingly seen in you. The grace that was given to you and the Spirit-deposit that is inside you inclines in this direction. It's as though you have swallowed a bag of iron filings (which, by the way, you should never do!) and

---

3 An illustration borrowed from a D.A. Carson sermon on this material.

now there is a strong attraction within you towards the magnetic call of the kingdom of heaven. As you are daily filled with God's grace, and as you are ever being filled with the Holy Spirit, you should be moving deeper into poverty of Spirit. You should feel an increasing disconnect with the ways of this world and an ever-deepening sorrow and concern for those in bondage to sin. The kingdom is in you; it is growing in you even as your heart cries, "Even so, come Lord Jesus."

When my son Max was nine years old, he decided that he wanted to be baptized. Excited as I was, I also wanted to be sure he was ready. I wanted to be sure he wasn't just doing this to make Dad happy or because his friend had done it or because it meant that he could stay upstairs at church once a month and take communion. I wanted to make sure he knew what he was communicating and what he was committing to.

I decided to have him memorize the beatitudes in Matthew 5. We spent about six weeks working on this as a family in Family Devotions until he had it down cold. Then, on Thanksgiving Day 2011, I took Max for a long walk and began peppering him with serious questions: "Max, do you know what it really means to be poor in spirit? Are you prepared to live that way by his grace? Will you let God be your God and let his Word be your truth for your whole life long? Will you live in a state of perpetual repentance and humility before him? Do you know what it means to be merciful? Will you live that out, even in the way you treat your sisters? Are you prepared to suffer for righteousness' sake? Do you understand that if you live out your Christian commitment fully, it may well cost you your life?"

It was a good walk, maybe the best I've ever had. We prayed together by a little bridge over Grey Owl Lake that God would grant Max the grace to walk this narrow way. I believe something was born in Max that day and I look forward to watching him work out his salvation with fear and trembling. I want to blow on those beautiful divine coals of saving grace until a fire of converted life rages in my son. I want that for me and I want that for my flock and I want that for you as you walk this narrow way. This is the call of Jesus. This is the blessed and eternal life. Let's explore it together.

Chapter One

Blessed Are the Poor in Spirit, for Theirs is Kingdom of Heaven

Put simply, the beatitudes are a description of what a saved person looks like. They are not a description of how to get saved, but rather point out the direction that saved people are growing. Saved people, because of God's grace inside of them, are moving in these directions and are correspondingly moving deeper into God's blessing and favour.

As the last Beatitude points out, they are also moving deeper into the hostility and antagonism of a fallen world in rebellion against its Creator. A careful reading of the beatitudes reveals what scholars call an *inclusio*—the first and last beatitudes end with the same promise: "theirs is the kingdom of heaven." This tells us that Jesus intended these beatitudes to serve as bookends on the whole and to speak to each other about the way and walk of the kingdom. Together they teach us that poverty of spirit is the prerequisite of salvation and persecution is the ultimate result of living a fully converted life upon this fallen earth. Nevertheless, we are blessed because this road is a kingdom road and, though all to the left and the right will fade away, this way endures into everlasting joy and abundance.

To be poor in Spirit is not simply to be poor, but neither can it be divorced from the analogy of physical poverty. Indeed, Luke records Jesus saying:

> Blessed are you who are poor, for yours is the kingdom of God. (Luke 6:20, ESV)

It seems likely that Jesus gave this sermon many times and that he was in the practice of switching between these related phrases in order to make a point: spiritual poverty is closely analogous, though not identical, to material poverty. What then does it mean to be "poor in spirit"?

The Greek phrase *hoi ptokhoi* implies being intellectually humble. In the Old Testament, there was a frequent association between humility and poverty, just as there was between wealth and arrogance. There are several righteous and humble rich men in the Bible and there are several passages which suggest some poor people are poor because they are lazy, but nevertheless Jesus makes use here of a common analogous relationship between poverty and humility. What Jesus is saying is very similar to what is recorded in Isaiah 66:2:

> But this is the one to whom I will look: he who is humble and contrite in spirit and trembles at my word. (Isaiah 66:2, ESV)

A person who is poor in Spirit is humble before God. He does not argue with God; he is instructed by him. He does not think himself wise enough to know good from evil, so he trusts in the Word of the Lord. He does not edit, shade, or critique the Word of God; he reads it, attends to it, and aligns with it in fear and trembling. This is the picture of the man to whom salvation comes. This is a picture of the blessed man.

A person like this is ideally positioned to receive the grace of God because he knows his need of it. He knows that all his righteous works fall pitifully short in view of God's goodness. He knows that his heart is deceitful above all things. He knows that he is too ignorant to make his own moral choices—he cannot know what the consequences will be for others and he cannot even know what the outcomes will be for himself. It is best to let the Lord speak and then simply obey. This is the man who has been given grace to be other than Adam.

But let us remember that poverty of spirit, as with all the beatitudes, does not describe how one becomes saved; it is a description of the saved man. The saved man is humble before God and is becoming all the more so. The fully converted person trusts implicitly the Word of God and is growing in that trust. No one is this way by nature. No one is born this way. No one becomes this way by natural means. It is only an encounter with the grace of God that leaves a person poor in spirit. It is only when God reveals himself to a proud and rebellious man that he falls to his knees and says, as Peter did:

> Go away from me, Lord, for I am a sinful man!
> (Luke 5:8)

Or as Isaiah said:

> Woe is me! I am lost, for I am a man of unclean lips, and I live among a people of unclean lips; yet

my eyes have seen the King, the Lord of hosts!
(Isaiah 6:5)

Poverty of spirit is the threshold of eternal life. It is, in this sense, both the precondition and the initial fruit of real conversion. Saving grace is both the help of God to apprehend salvation and the gift of God that is itself given. Poverty of spirit is the help that God gives so that a person can take hold of the gift of salvation. A proud man sees no need of salvation; he thinks himself good enough already. A rich man feels secure and gives little thought to his eternal peril. A wise man thinks he knows a few things the simple "religious folks" are ignorant of and will trust his teachers and his books. A man who is spiritually poor knows he doesn't know. He knows he is not secure and he knows he is not nearly good enough. This is the one who is ready to be blessed. Indeed, this is the one who has already been blessed. He has been pressed down by the hand of God and has found the doggy-door to eternal life.

The Bible is a wonderful mix of proposition and story. Some of us deal better in one than in the other, so let me illustrate this proposition—*"blessed are the poor in spirit, for theirs is the kingdom of heaven"*—with a teaching of Jesus, given in story. In Luke 18, Jesus had been talking about how saved people pray and then he told a story to tell who saved people are. The story is about two men:

> Two men went up into the temple to pray, one a Pharisee and the other a tax collector. The Pharisee, standing by himself, prayed thus: "God, I thank you that I am not like other men, extortioners, unjust, adulterers, or even like this tax collector. I fast twice a week; I give tithes of all that I get."
>
> But the tax collector, standing far off, would not even lift up his eyes to heaven, but beat his

breast, saying, "God, be merciful to me, a sinner!" I tell you, this man went down to his house justified, rather than the other. For everyone who exalts himself will be humbled, but the one who humbles himself will be exalted. (Luke 18:10–14, ESV)

Jesus explains who the saved people are by means of a story comparing these two men. The first man is a Pharisee. The first thing we are told about the Pharisee is that he stood and prayed with himself. That's an odd phrase, but it means to communicate something along the lines of "he held himself aloof," as we used to say in English. The idea is that this man held himself closer to God than to men. He thought himself pretty much equal to God and far above other people. He was proud and self-satisfied. He was proud of the fact that he had overcome regular human vices and that he excelled in acts of religious piety. He says to God, "Not only do I not commit adultery, but I fast far more often than the Bible says I need to and I tithe on things the Bible says I don't need to! I am really a wonderful man!" In the Bible, there are only a few set days for fasting and at that time many Jews had gone so far as to fast once a week, but this fellow had doubled their efforts and fasted *twice* a week! In terms of tithing, a man was supposed to tithe on his income, but he was not required to tithe on his purchases. The Greek word used here is *ktomai,* and it means "I acquire." What this means is that when he was buying something—say, a donkey—he was tithing ten percent of the purchase price. Now, the law just said that the seller had to tithe on the sale price, because that was his income, but this guy is saying, "Lord, because I can't be sure whether or not this filthy miscreant is tithing on this transaction, I shall tithe on the purchase side so that the item may be holy, as indeed I am holy." Arrogant, self-satisfied, holier than thou, holier than necessary; this is the Pharisee. He is the opposite of the tax collector.

The tax collector stood far off. That probably means he stood in the court of the Gentiles. This guy was so repentant, so filled with anguish over his sin, that he counted himself a Gentile rather than a Jew. He felt cut off from God because of his sin. He wouldn't dare to even raise his eyes when he prayed; rather, he beat his breast with his fist. The chest was viewed as the seat of sin and this man *hated* the sin he saw in his own heart. He dared not cite any act of righteousness to God and instead said something *wildly* profound. What he said cannot be translated into English. Our Bibles have him saying "Have mercy on me," but that doesn't quite get it. He uses the word *hilastheiti*, which means "become propitious" towards me. It is the word that lies at the centre of Paul's Gospel presentation in Romans 3:

> For all have sinned and fall short of the glory of God, being justified freely by His grace through the redemption that is in Christ Jesus, *whom God set forth as a propitiation by His blood,* through faith, to demonstrate His righteousness, because in His forbearance God had passed over the sins that were previously committed, to demonstrate at the present time His righteousness, that He might be just and the justifier of the one who has faith in Jesus. *Where is boasting then? It is excluded.* (Romans 3:23–27, NKJV, emphasis mine)

This tax collector cries out to God asking for propitiation! He asks for God to somehow deal with the wrath that he so justly deserves, such that he can see God's favour and mercy. He doesn't know how this can occur. He doesn't know *how a holy God* can love a man like him, but he cries out for God to find a way! He knows that if God finds such a way, if God does such a miracle, it will be no cause for human boasting. He will have contributed *nothing*. God will have done the impossible; God will have done a *miracle* on his behalf. That is the substance of Gospel faith, my friend. That is poverty of spirit in a nutshell, and Jesus says:

> This man went down to his house *justified*. (Luke 18:14, NKJV, emphasis mine)

This is what it means to be saved! This is the heart of the Gospel! This is the one who inherits the kingdom of heaven. Indeed, this one begins to walk in it even now! This is the one who is lifted up on the last day, the one who is pressed face down before God all the days that come before!

Christianity is, at its heart, a daily journey of repentance. It is a daily process of hating the sin we see in our own hearts and looking to a holy God to provide for that which separates us from his divine presence. Too often, we speak of repentance as though it were only something associated with the start of our Christian journey—though sometimes we ignore it then, too. Often we speak as though repentance is something for the first day of the Christian journey and then move on to joy and confidence, but that leads to the false assurance of the Pharisee! He was so proud of his overcoming. Christian friends, can't you see the warning in this? I do.

When I was a young man, I struggled with the things all young men struggle with: anger and lust. I would beat my breast over those things before God, *hating* the sin I saw in my own heart. In my twenties, I would cry out to God, day after day, night after night, holding myself far off and fearing to lift my eyes to gaze upon his holy face. But now, as I approach the hump of life and begin to head down the other side, there is such a temptation to feel arrogant and proud. I no longer struggle with those things "like other men." I haven't punched someone in the face in fifteen years, I'm happily married and colouring inside the lines in terms of human sexuality, and I've got kids all over the place! But now my faith is assaulted by Pharisaic pride! It's so easy, in our maturity, to become arrogant and to despise those who struggle with things we've left behind because of former graces given to us by the hand of God! Younger people, beat your breast over the sin in your hearts until God grants you grace and liberty. Older people, *press yourselves down* before the God who gave you grace and liberty. Do not raise yourself up and hold yourself closer to God than other men. All of Christianity is a daily walk of repentance and lowliness and persevering prayer until the end. This is poverty of spirit. Blessed are the poor in Spirit, for theirs is the kingdom of heaven.

The Kingdom of Heaven

In each of the beatitudes, there is a connection made between an aspect of the fully converted life and what might be best called an "eschatological promise." The word "eschatology" sounds more impressive than it is. It simply means "relating to the end." Each aspect of the fully converted life lived *now* is connected to some promise of the end. As with most eschatological promises, there is a sense in which the thing promised will be realized in an ultimate sense after the Second Coming and the Renewal of all things. Simultaneously, there is a sense in which we have the first fruits, the initial experience as it were, of the thing promised in the here and now.

This beatitude promises: *"for theirs is the kingdom of heaven."* As we mentioned earlier, this first beatitude forms an inclusion with the eighth; they share an eschatological promise. They are tied to our inheriting the kingdom. There is a sense in which we inherit and occupy the kingdom now. We are citizens of heaven, we have our names written in the Lamb's Book of Life, and we are partakers of the divine glory. But there is a much fuller sense in which those things will be realized in the age to come. Because this promise is repeated in the eight beatitude, we will unpack it in greater detail at that time. For now it is enough to remember that poverty of spirit is the threshold of kingdom life. No one enters the kingdom accept that he enters on his knees. The Bible says:

> God opposes the proud, but gives grace to the humble. (James 4:6, ESV)

Small Group Discussion

It is likely true that nothing else in the Sermon on the Mount makes sense until you have figured out what Jesus means by being "poor in spirit." Let's read the texts below before addressing the comprehension task that follows.

Luke 6:20, 24
Mark 10:17–31
Isaiah 57:15
Philippians 3:7–1
Philippians 2:5–11
Luke 5:8

Comprehension Task: Take a moment to consider the twelve statements below. Circle all that you think correctly reflect the teaching of Jesus on being "poor in spirit."

1. There is no one in the kingdom of God who is not poor in spirit.

2. All the other characteristics cited in these beatitudes are in a sense the result of this first one.
3. To be poor in spirit means that a person is shy, weak, and lacking in strength and courage.
4. Being poor in spirit is fundamentally about being empty of worldly things and values. We cannot be filled with the things of heaven until we have been emptied of the things of earth.
5. The Christian life begins with the fundamental understanding that you bring nothing to it. Grace is required to begin and to walk this narrow way.
6. It is better to be poor than to be rich. God is opposed to those with material abundance.
7. To be materially poor is a blessing because it humbles the soul and disciplines us. Material wealth can make us proud and place a barrier between us and the grace of God.
8. Those who approach the narrow gate with no earthly possessions are actually in a much better position than those who approach heavily loaded with worldly things.
9. The way to become poor in spirit is to look at God. The more we see Christ, with the aid of the Holy Spirit, we will either reject him or be deeply humbled.
10. The North American spirit of independence, self-reliance and idealisation of prosperity is in general harmony with this beatitude.
11. If God wanted to start a revival in North America, it might be helpful to send another Great Depression. Maybe if our wealth was taken, we would find ourselves closer to the narrow gate of salvation.
12. If I put any faith in my wealth, my natural gifts, my education, or any other form of human (fleshly) advantage, I am not poor in spirit and I am not placing saving faith in Christ.

Personal Reflection and Evaluation

There is a great danger in studying a passage of Scripture such as this and then simply moving on in order to learn "the next new thing." The Bible says:

> But be doers of the word, and not merely hearers who deceive themselves. For if any are hearers of the word and not doers, they are like those who look at themselves in a mirror; for they look at themselves and, on going away, immediately forget what they were like. But those who look into the perfect law, the law of liberty, and persevere, being not hearers who forget but doers who act— *they will be blessed in their doing.* (James 1:22–25, emphasis mine)

The Sermon on the Mount is a description of what a Christian should look like. The beatitudes are a description of a fully converted person. Therefore, we would be the greatest of fools not to ask a simple follow-up question: "To what extent do I look this way?" Some fear that this will lead to legalism. They suppose that to apply a teaching is to suggest that one may "earn salvation" by finding oneself in alignment with the principle that is being taught. But that is ridiculous! The law does not make for salvation, whether the Old Testament version or "the new commandment" of Jesus. Jesus does not say, "Live this way and you will be saved." He says, "Christians live this way, by grace, and are blessed, both now and in the age to come."

The Sermon on the Mount is also meant to drive us to salvation. It sets such an impossibly high standard that the man of the flesh (the unsaved person) reads it and is driven to his knees in search of grace, forgiveness, and empowerment. It is meant to be an otherworldly standard. If in taking this assessment you discover that you feel overwhelmed and wretched, wracked with guilt and a sense of failure, praise the Lord! You are simply in need of saving grace. Please contact your small group leader immediately.

A Christian using this reflection and evaluation tool might be tempted to give himself a "grace-based pass." He or she may say to herself, "Christianity is, of course, above all things, a way of grace. I ought not expect that I should score high on all of these markers. I am in process and this is an ideal standard." Unfortunately, that is not quite true. Jesus said:

> For I tell you, unless your righteousness exceeds that of the scribes and Pharisees, you will never enter the kingdom of heaven. (Matthew 5:20)

The New Testament uniformly teaches that if you are truly saved, if the Holy Spirit is truly in you, then the fruit of the Spirit will be *increasingly manifest* (shown to be present) within your life. The fruit of the Spirit, you will notice, looks an awful lot like the beatitudes. If you use this evaluation tool and discover that your fruit is looking rather bruised and faded, you need to follow the Apostle Paul's example, who said:

> I die daily. (1 Corinthians 15:31)

The enemy was constantly at work in Paul's life, trying to sow back in the fruit of the flesh. Paul acknowledges that he waged a lifelong battle with pride, which is the opposite of being poor in spirit. He knew that he had to die every day to his pride and his dependence upon his great intellect, outstanding education, Roman citizenship, and Jewish lineage. To rely or find identity in any of those things was to cultivate the fruit of the flesh. He had to die to them everyday so that the fruit of the Spirit would grow, so that he could be blessed of God and walk in grace.

As a Christian, you may discover that you need to die again and again and again. This is the very act of spiritual emptying that allows you to be filled. Do not despise it or disbelieve it. All Christians should be characterised by *all* of these beatitudes in ever-increasing degree. What is impossible in the flesh is possible by the Spirit and through grace. If you score poorly, simply humble yourself, repent, and seek grace. We don't stop seeking grace after we are saved. Rather, we seek it all the more. We call this sanctification and it's not a myth, a relic, or a rumour. It is the narrow way. If you barely register on these as we go through, you need to read the epilogue immediately and discuss it with your small group leader.

Take some time and carefully consider the following ten statements. If the statement is *always true of you,* then give yourself a score of ten. If it is *sometimes true of you,* give yourself a five. If it is *rarely or never true of you,* give yourself a zero. Tally your score out of a hundred when you have completed the exercise.

1. When I consider God, either in prayerful contemplation or in my reading of the Scriptures, I am overwhelmed with his rightness, goodness, and holiness. I am filled with gratitude for his unwarranted grace to me.
2. When I consider myself, I am deeply aware of how far from the standard of the cross I have lived. I am so aware that I have no intrinsic merit, no personal worth that explains God's love for me.
3. I derive none of my personal worth from my wealth, my worldly success or positions, my education, or my family background.
4. My identity comes from being a saved son or daughter of God through Jesus Christ. Every other label or form of identity means nothing to me.

5. I never boast in my possessions or accomplishments. Whether they are noticed or appreciated by the world is not my concern.
6. My conversation is dominated by words of gratitude for God's grace and reflections on his goodness, holiness, and justice.
7. I measure myself against the cross, not the crowd, other believers, or not the Joneses next door.
8. I believe *deeply* in the grace of God and the empowerment of the Holy Spirit. I believe that all things are possible for those who believe. I believe that by his Spirit I can do "these and greater things."
9. I look forward to receiving from God's hand whatever blessing he has in store for me in eternity. Earthly riches have no interest to me, other than as a means of advancing the kingdom.
10. My life and my schedule are not cluttered with the things of this world. All of my time, all of my treasure, all of my breath and waking life is at the disposal of Almighty God. "Here am I, Lord, send me" is my humble cry.

My score out of 100: _____

Evaluated on this date: _____

My prayer of honest response to the Lord:

_____

_____

_____

_____

_____

_____

Frequently Asked Questions

Early on in my ministry, I heard a useful saying: "Pastoral ministry is the fine art of answering the same 50 questions 10,000 times." The beauty of walking the narrow way is that you are travelling a well-worn path. Many people have gone this way before, asked, and by God's grace answered most of the questions you are asking as you go.

When we first published *Mile 1*, we included all of the most commonly asked questions from having used the material in small groups prior to forming the content into a book. The process of creating *The Narrow Way* has been slightly different and as such we've decided to handle the FAQ a little differently this time around. We have collected several FAQs for each chapter and posted them at our website. You can track with them as you read by visiting www.beaconcitypublishing.com.

Additionally, you can post questions as you read that I will attempt to answer, or if the volume does not allow, I will get a veteran small group user to address. Please post any questions you may have, as it allows us to better serve those who benefit from these resources.

Chapter Two

Blessed Are Those Who Mourn, for They Will be Comforted

Let us recall that the beatitudes are a description of what a saved person looks like. They are not a description of how to get saved, but rather they point out the direction that truly converted people are growing in. Saved people, because of God's grace inside of them, are moving in these directions and are correspondingly moving deeper into God's blessing and deeper into the hostility and rejection of the world. As a person moves deeper into the things of God, they are moving out of the things of the world. When a person is truly converted, there is an immediate change of citizenship and affiliation. The Bible says things like:

> Our citizenship is in heaven. (Philippians 3:20)

> He has rescued us from the power of darkness and transferred us into the kingdom of his beloved Son. (Colossians 1:13)

When a person becomes a Christian, they begin to live in a new space—a kingdom space—and they increasingly depart from the things of this dying world. With each passing day, they feel less at home, less comfortable, and less "native" to the ways of this earth. A Christian is not to try and stay "in love" with the world; he is to love the world to come.

> Do not love the world or the things in the world. The love of the Father is not in those who love the world; for all that is in the world—the desire of the flesh, the desire of the eyes, the pride in riches—comes not from the Father but from the world. And the world and its desire are passing away, but those who do the will of God live for ever. (1 John 2:15–17)

A saved person stops loving the world. Of course they love the people in the world, but that is not the same thing. John tells us what we are to stop loving—the desire of the flesh, the desire of the eyes, the pride in riches; these worldly things are seen increasingly by the saved person as the source of all sin, all rebellion, all arrogance, all pain, all mischief, all injury, and all the death that is truly characteristic of this present darkness.

A saved person mourns that which he once loved. He cannot laugh at the movies he once thought so funny. He sees now through a different lens. He cannot take pleasure in the things he once found so enjoyable. He has a new set of values and he understands now the vanity in such things. The things he would once have called hobbies he would now label as bondage. The things he would once have called distractions he now sees as deceptions. The things he would once have called entertainments he would now call idolatries. He feels strangely out of tune with the music of the world and he cannot find his feet to dance.

This is a wonderful and dangerous place in the walk of faith. Wonderful, because it is the place where other hungers are born. The hunger for the Word of God is often born or intensified in this place. The hunger for worship is found here, as is the hope of eternity. Dangerous, because this can so easily become judgementalism and depression. Mourning is not hate, anger, isolationism, or fatalism. It is realism. It is prophetic. It is urgency and it is courage. The truly converted Christian who knows how deceptive and enslaving are the things of this world, and who knows well what glories and what pleasures are reserved for him in heaven, wades boldly into the roiling sea and rescues every soul he can lay hold of. He does not fear the loss of his life, for this world has lost its hold on him. He is motivated by both pity and informed ambition. He recalls that Jesus said:

> Do not store up for yourselves treasures on earth, where moth and rust consume and where thieves break in and steal; but store up for yourselves treasures in heaven, where neither moth nor rust consumes and where thieves do not break in and steal. For where your treasure is, there your heart will be also. (Matthew 6:19–21)

It's not that he has no taste for treasure; it's that he has no taste for *earthly* treasure. He longs to be comforted by the good things that are given at the hand of God to those servants who have been faithful while he tarried. Theologians refer to this as the recompense; the same Hebrew word in Isaiah 61:2 that is translated as "comfort" can be translated as "recompense." It means to sooth hurts and to punish wrongs. It means to reward right and damn evil. Coming to Jesus does not make a man poor; it makes a man newly rich. He leaves behind the things he no longer values and moves into new and enduring treasures that will neither tarnish nor fade. In another giving of this sermon, Jesus said:

> Then he looked up at his disciples and said: "Blessed are you who are poor, for yours is the kingdom of God… Blessed are you who weep now, for you will laugh… But woe to you who are rich, for you have received your consolation… Woe to you who are laughing now, for you will mourn and weep. (Luke 6:20–21, 24–25)

The point Jesus seems to be making is that it is a terrible tragedy when a man develops a taste for the "good things" of this world. They taste sweet in the mouth, but they poison the stomach. They lead to death, weeping, and mourning in the world to come. On the contrary, it is a good thing, a blessed thing, to lose your taste for this world, to see its utter barrenness and depravity. The hunger and sadness you feel here will press you forward into the good things of God. Your best life is yet to come, and what a glorious life it will be!

Mourning in the Bible is not just a wise thing, a good thing, or even a mark of spiritual maturity. When people mourn, when they sigh and grieve over sin, they give evidence that they understand the gravity of sin and the offense that it represents against the holiness of God. It marks them as the people of God. Ezekiel 9 contains a rather chilling prophetic word:

Then he cried in my ears with a loud voice, saying, "Bring near the executioners of the city, each with his destroying weapon in his hand."

And behold, six men came from the direction of the upper gate, which faces north, each with his weapon for slaughter in his hand, and with them was a man clothed in linen, with a writing case at his waist. And they went in and stood beside the bronze altar.

Now the glory of the God of Israel had gone up from the cherub on which it rested to the threshold of the house. And he called to the man clothed in linen, who had the writing case at his waist.

And the Lord said to him, "Pass through the city, through Jerusalem, *and put a mark on the foreheads of the men who sigh and groan over all the abominations that are committed in it.*" And to the others he said in my hearing, "Pass through the city after him, and strike. Your eye shall not spare, and you shall show no pity. Kill old men outright, young men and maidens, little children and women, but touch no one on whom is the mark. And begin at my sanctuary." *So they began with the elders who were before the house.* Then he said to them, "Defile the house, and fill the courts with the slain. Go out." So they went out and struck in the city.

And while they were striking, and I was left alone, I fell upon my face, and cried, "Ah, Lord God! Will you destroy all the remnant of Israel in the outpouring of your wrath on Jerusalem?"

Then he said to me, "The guilt of the house of Israel and Judah is exceedingly great. *The land is full of blood, and the city full of injustice.* For they say, 'The Lord has forsaken the land, and the Lord does not see.' As for me, my eye will not spare, nor will I have pity; I will bring their deeds upon their heads."

And behold, the man clothed in linen, with the writing case at his waist, brought back word, saying, "I have done as you commanded me." (Ezekiel 9:1–11, ESV, emphasis mine)

Did you read that story carefully? God is going to visit devastating wrath upon the nation of Israel, but before he does he sends out an angel to mark off the true remnant, the true Israel, the truly converted people of God. What sets them apart from the rest? How does the angel recognise them against the backdrop of all sorts of people who claim to be religious, who profess the Lord's name with their lips and who bear on their bodies the external marks of the covenant? How does he know who the remnant are that should be saved from the wrath of the Lord? They are the ones who sigh and groan over all the abominations that are committed in their city. They are those who mourn. Scholars generally agree that this passage stands behind Peter's warning in 1 Peter 4, where he says:

> For it is time for judgment to begin at the household of God; and if it begins with us, what will be the outcome for those who do not obey the gospel of God? And "If the righteous is scarcely saved, what will become of the ungodly and the sinner?" (1 Peter 4:17–18, ESV)

Did you notice that in Ezekiel 9 the angel with the marker went *first* to investigate the elders who were before the house? That's why

Peter moves immediately from this teaching to a lengthy teaching on eldership. The point is that it doesn't matter if you are a member of the people of God in an external sense. It doesn't matter if you are circumcised or baptized. It doesn't even matter if you are an *elder in the church!* The proof that you are truly saved is that you *mourn* over idolatry, abomination, and injustice!

Man looks on the outward signs, but God looks on the *heart!* Does your heart truly grieve over the consequences of sin? Does your heart laugh at things that actually hold created people in bondage to sin and death? Do you find entertaining or do you find disinteresting the things in your culture that are condemning men and women to *hell*? God looks in your heart to see if there is brokenness there! Jesus was a man of sorrows, and the Bible records him crying but never laughing. That is not to say that humour is a sin; it's just to say that tears are characteristic of the truly converted. It is an honest, tearful apprehension of the lostness of the world that marks off the remnant from the rest. Blessed are those who mourn, for they shall be comforted at the recompense of Almighty God.

They Shall Be Comforted

As mentioned previously, in each of the beatitudes there is a connection made between an aspect of the fully converted life and what might be best called an "eschatological promise." Each aspect of the fully converted life lived *now* is connected to some promise of the end. As with most eschatological promises, there is a sense in which the thing promised will be realized in an ultimate sense after the Second Coming and the Renewal of all things. Simultaneously, there is a sense in which we have the first fruits, the down payment, the initial experience of the thing promised in the here and now. This beatitude promises: *"for they shall be comforted."* The Greek word here is *parakaleo* and it is related to a word sometimes used to describe the Holy Spirit as in John 14:

> But the Comforter, which is the Holy Ghost, whom the Father will send in my name, he shall teach you all things, and bring all things to your remembrance, whatsoever I have said unto you. (John 14:26, KJV)

That word ("the Comforter") is the Greek *parakletos*, and you can easily see how they are related. Thus the promised blessing seems to be that those who mourn, those who despise idolatry, abomination (things hateful to God), and injustice will be given the Holy Spirit. This will comfort us because we will see growing in us the things of life even as we live among the things of death. This is why Paul presents the fruit of the spirit the way he does, in the context of the fruits of death:

> But I say, walk by the Spirit, and you will not gratify the desires of the flesh. For the desires of the flesh are against the Spirit, and the desires of the Spirit are against the flesh, for these are opposed to each other, to keep you from doing the things you want to do. But if you are led by the Spirit, you are not under the law. Now the works of the flesh are evident: sexual immorality, impurity, sensuality, idolatry, sorcery, enmity, strife, jealousy, fits of anger, rivalries, dissensions, divisions, envy, drunkenness, orgies, and things like these. I warn you, as I warned you before, that those who do such things will not inherit the kingdom of God. But the fruit of the Spirit is love, joy, peace, patience,

kindness, goodness, faithfulness, gentleness, self-control; against such things there is no law. And those who belong to Christ Jesus have crucified the flesh with its passions and desires. If we live by the Spirit, let us also walk by the Spirit. (Galatians 5:16–25, ESV)

The fruit of the Spirit grow in fully converted hearts even as they live among the fruits of death that break their hearts. Those who mourn are given first fruits and deposits of the Holy Spirit that serve to teach us truth (which comforts us) and to work out beautiful character through us. The Holy Spirit also gives us gifts that allow us to work effectively to save men and women from the things we hate that are working death in them:

> Now there are varieties of gifts, but the same Spirit; and there are varieties of service, but the same Lord; and there are varieties of activities, but it is the same God who empowers them all in everyone. To each is given the manifestation of the Spirit for the common good. To one is given through the Spirit the utterance of wisdom, and to another the utterance of knowledge according to the same Spirit, to another faith by the same Spirit, to another gifts of healing by the one Spirit, to another the working of miracles, to another prophecy, to another the ability to distinguish between spirits, to another various kinds of tongues, to another the interpretation of tongues. All these are empowered by one and the same Spirit, who apportions to each one individually as he wills. (1 Corinthians 12:4–11, ESV)

By means of these gifts, we are able to minister collectively to people who are lost, enslaved, and being destroyed by the effects of sin. This is a comfort to those who truly mourn over the state of unsaved men and women. These are first fruit comforts and are given to those who are truly converted. We know, however, that a greater share in the things of the Spirit awaits us in the age to come. In this same section of Scripture, Paul said:

> As for prophecies, they will pass away; as for tongues, they will cease; as for knowledge, it will pass away. For we know in part and we prophesy in part, but when the perfect comes, the partial will pass away. When I was a child, I spoke like a child, I thought like a child, I reasoned like a child. When I became a man, I gave up childish ways. For now we see in a mirror dimly, but then face to face. Now I know in part; then I shall know fully, even as I have been fully known. (1 Corinthians 13:8–12, ESV)

All of these gifts that help comfort us now will be far surpassed by the things yet to come. Prophesy is very helpful now, and tongues can be a wonderful encouragement, but they will all pass away just as the light of stars passes away when the sun comes out in the morning. Now we are encouraged in part. Then we shall be fully known. We shall see him face to face and it will be enough.

That, of course, is the great climactic promise of Scripture, that we shall see God face to face. In fact, the Book of Revelation borrows imagery from Ezekiel 9 in order to give us that encouragement. After the Second Coming, John describes a most encouraging vision:

> Then I saw thrones, and seated on them were those to whom the authority to judge was committed. Also I saw the souls of those who had been beheaded for the testimony of Jesus and for the word of God, and who had not worshiped the beast or its image and *had not received its mark on their foreheads* or their hands. They came to life and reigned with Christ for a thousand years. The rest of the dead did not come to life until the thousand years were ended. This is the first resurrection. Blessed and holy is the one who shares in the first resurrection! Over such the second death has no power, but they will be priests of God and of Christ, and they will reign with him for a thousand years. (Revelation 20:4–6, ESV, emphasis mine)

Throughout the Book of Revelation, which is full of end-time promises, we see people being marked with various marks. Everyone by the end has received one of two: they either bear the mark of the beast or the mark of the Lamb. Scholars generally agree that this imagery is borrowed wholesale from Ezekiel 9. Those who receive the mark of the Lamb are those who have mourned over sin and the hateful, God-dishonouring things that are going on all around them. Those who take the mark of the beast are those who are seduced into all manner of idolatry. Those who have mourned are raised to reign. They are recompensed. They are comforted. Later it is said of them:

> They will see his face, and his name will be on their foreheads. And night will be no more. They will need no light of lamp or sun, for the Lord God will be their light, and they will reign forever and ever. (Revelation 22:4–5, ESV)

The blessing upon those who mourn begins now, but it gets better and better until it can get no more glorious. They shall see his face and his name shall be on their foreheads. The Lord will be their light and they shall reign forever and ever. Blessed be the name!

Small Group Discussion

The second beatitude says, *"Blessed are those who mourn, for they shall be comforted."* There has been precious little teaching on this beatitude in the church over the last hundred years. Many commentators suggest that this is due in part to a reaction against the false puritanism of the nineteenth century. Many Christians felt that acting dour and sombre and condemning all expressions of joy and happiness somehow made them more like Jesus. As society tired of this, the pendulum in Christendom swung fully in the other direction, making glib, inauthentic blissfulness the order of the day.

Now pastors with megawatt smiles, artificially whitened to an alarming degree, tell us how to be constantly happy and blissful, enjoying our best lives now. Hmm. Yet Jesus was called a man of sorrows, and while he is often found weeping, he is *never* once found laughing in all of Scripture. What are we to make of this? What does it mean to "mourn"? Let's read the texts below and then address the comprehension task that follows.

Matthew 5:4
Luke 6:21, 25
Isaiah 53:3
Luke 19:41–44
John 11:33–36
Romans 7:21–25
Romans 8:22–23

2 Corinthians 5:2–5
Titus 2:1-8
1 Timothy 3:8, 11
Romans 8:18
Revelation 21:1–5

Comprehension Task: Take a moment to consider the twelve statements below. Circle all that you think correctly reflect the teaching of Jesus on being one "who mourns."

1. Being one who mourns begins with a deep awareness of one's own sins. Conviction must precede conversion. If there is no sorrow over sin, one cannot be saved.
2. After a person has been truly saved, they will no longer mourn. "Blessed are those who mourn" applies only to those in the process of getting saved.
3. A true Christian is often, even perpetually, mourning over the sinful tendencies in his own life. He mourns his natural greed, his natural lust, and his natural pride that constantly threaten to separate him from the will of God and the peaceful fellowship of his fellow man.
4. Only a Christian man or woman who maintains deep sorrow over the lingering stench of sin in his or her own life can know true joy over the wonder of salvation and the grace of true forgiveness. They know the answer to the question: who will rescue me from this body of death?
5. Part of the reason why so few are walking the narrow way and enjoying the blessings of the Holy Spirit is that many churches no longer preach the truth about sin. We don't want people to feel guilty. As a result, they are often not truly saved and often lack in gratitude for the work of the cross.

6. The one who mourns also grieves over the sin of others. He mourns its effects, its cost, and its ultimate consequence. He does not simply condemn; he mourns.
7. The one who mourns does not feel at peace in this world. She recognises the pervasive and creeping influence of sin upon all aspects of the world. She is deeply disturbed and sober in reflection.
8. The best course of action according to Jesus is to not dwell on all the negatives. Avoid watching the news, focus on the positive, and build your best life now, by God's grace.
9. It is wrong for a Christian to laugh, tell jokes, or to be happy.
10. A true Christian, one who mourns, is willing to pay the price in order to follow God's will and minister to the lost. He knows that this life, hard as it is, foreign as it feels, will be brief and the glories of eternity many and long lasting.
11. A true Christian is focused on leisure pursuits in the here and now. Boating, fishing, and all manner of amusements and distractions help kill time while we wait for the Rapture.
12. A true Christian is fuelled in her ministry by a vision of the eternal kingdom, when all wounds are healed and all sorrows lifted.

Personal Reflection and Evaluation

As mentioned previously, there is a great danger in studying a passage of Scripture such as this and then simply moving on in order to learn "the next new thing." The Bible says:

> But be doers of the word, and not merely hearers who deceive themselves. For if any are hearers of

the word and not doers, they are like those who look at themselves in a mirror; for they look at themselves and, on going away, immediately forget what they were like. But those who look into the perfect law, the law of liberty, and persevere, being not hearers who forget but doers who act— *they will be blessed in their doing.* (James 1:22–25, emphasis mine)

The Sermon on the Mount is a description of what *every* Christian should look like. We would be the greatest of fools not to ask a simple follow-up question: "To what extent do I look this way?"

Take some time to carefully consider the following ten statements. If the statement is *always true of you,* give yourself a score of ten. If it is *sometimes true of you,* give yourself a five. If it is *rarely or never true of you,* give yourself a zero. Tally your score out of a hundred when you have completed the exercise.

1. I am fully aware and one hundred percent convinced that I am unworthy of God's grace and consideration. I am a sinful man/woman and am unfit, but for his grace, for the presence of Almighty God.
2. I practice rigorous self-examination and am aware of the continuing influence and stain of sin upon my life. I feel the pull of old addictions, recognise the flares of old angers and the temptation of old pride. I mourn the distance between my present disposition and my original, created nature.
3. I wish I were free from all pull of sin, all call of pride, so that I could worship God better and live more peacefully with my fellow man.
4. I am so thankful for the grace of God applied to my account through faith in the life, death, and resurrection of

Jesus Christ! His blood has made me *holy in standing* before Almighty God. Praise the Lord!
5. I constantly seek the holiness and righteousness of God through studying the Scriptures and contemplation of the example of Jesus Christ so that I can experience growth and sanctification. I want to be like the Lord!
6. I hate what sin is doing to the people of this city. I loathe addiction, I despise lust, I abhor greed, I and would stab the devil in the eye with a fork if ever given the chance. I deeply desire to see people free from sin so that they could enjoy their Creator and live at peace with their fellow man.
7. I am deeply troubled by the state of the world. I see the sinister, corrosive influence of sin in all aspects of our global society. I see it in the corruption of politicians, the hedonism of athletes and actors, the hypocrisy and weakness of the clergy, the ignorance of the masses, and the selfishness and deceitfulness of the media.
8. I do not feel at home in this world. I often feel out of step and out of the loop. I do not laugh at the jokes my neighbours think are funny and I am not amused by the things they are amused with. This doesn't feel right to me.
9. I am aware that life is short and glory is long. On this time I have on earth, I want to do what I can, by God's grace, to bless and serve and advance the Gospel. I am very focused on my ministry and calling, whatever that may be. I am not distracted by leisure or worldly entanglements, as though this world was my home.
10. My vision of heaven sustains me when I suffer in this world. I have a great longing for the eternal kingdom and a great desire to see all things under the wise leadership of Jesus Christ.

Blessed Are Those Who Mourn

My score out of 100: _____

Evaluated on this date: _____

My prayer of honest response to the Lord:

_____

_____

_____

_____

_____

_____

Chapter Three

Blessed Are the Meek, for They Will Inherit the Earth

Meekness may be the most misunderstood word in the Bible. Maybe that's because it sounds like "weakness," or maybe it's because it is so rarely spoken of or modelled in the world today. Happily, an entire chapter of the Old Testament is dedicated to extending definition of this word, which Jesus is obviously drawing upon. Scholars agree that Jesus is here referencing Psalm 37, which is an extended commentary on the life of meekness. Indeed the climax of the chapter declares:

> But the meek shall inherit the earth, and shall delight themselves in the abundance of peace. (Psalm 37:11, NKJV)

The people listening to Jesus give this sermon wouldn't have missed that, and neither should we. When you read Psalm 37, it becomes clear that the Psalmist is contrasting the meek man with the evildoer. The evildoer is envious of others. He lives for the moment without considering future consequences. He schemes and plots to advance himself at the expense of others. He is willing to make use of violence and fraud to accumulate wealth and power. He borrows money but walks away from his debts. He is wealthy and increasingly powerful, but it is all doomed to fail. Eventually and ultimately, his empire of lies and blood collapses and he meets his maker and is forced to account for his sins. The end of that man is ruin and darkness.

Not so, the man of meekness. His approach to life *begins* with an anticipation of the final reckoning. He knows that life on this earth is brief and that afterwards there is an accounting. He knows it is better to be poor for a lifetime and rich in eternity. He knows that the Lord sees all and knows all and he lives within the boundaries, seeking the things that make for peace and the pleasure of the Lord. His life plan is to please the Lord now and to be blessed of the Lord later. He is not angry when his plans don't succeed, because he knows the Lord's plan always prospers. He feels no frustration when his ambitions are thwarted because he knows that he shall ultimately inherit the earth in the kingdom of God. He does not panic or compromise in times of economic difficulty, because he trusts the Lord to provide. He does not change his giving patterns when things are tough, because the cattle on a thousand hills are God's. He studies the Word of God so as to live life in a pleasing and upright manner, believing this to be the path to peace and ultimate prosperity. He is no reed shaken by the wind, nor one disturbed by rumours or changes in the chambers of power and earthly influence. His trust is in the Lord. He knows not what the future may hold, but he knows the one who holds his future. This is the way of meekness.

The Old Testament goes to great lengths to commend this virtue to us and holds up several examples of how this looks in a well-lived life. Maybe the best two examples would be Abraham and David. Abraham knew that God had made him promises and that God kept his promises, so he didn't feel the need to fight and scrap and scheme for every advantage. Do you remember when he and his relative Lot parted company? Lot was the junior partner in this enterprise and yet look at the meekness of Abraham:

> Now Lot, who went with Abram, also had flocks and herds and tents, so that the land could not support both of them living together; for their possessions were so great that they could not live together, and there was strife between the herders of Abram's livestock and the herders of Lot's livestock. At that time the Canaanites and the Perizzites lived in the land.
>
> Then Abram said to Lot, "Let there be no strife between you and me, and between your herders and my herders; for we are kindred. Is not the whole land before you? Separate yourself from me. If you take the left hand, then I will go to the right; or if you take the right hand, then I will go to the left."
>
> Lot looked about him, and saw that the plain of the Jordan was well watered everywhere like the garden of the Lord, like the land of Egypt, in the direction of Zoar; this was before the Lord had destroyed Sodom and Gomorrah. So Lot chose for himself all the plain of the Jordan, and Lot journeyed eastwards; thus they separated from each other.
>
> Abram settled in the land of Canaan, while Lot settled among the cities of the Plain and moved

his tent as far as Sodom. Now the people of Sodom were wicked, great sinners against the Lord.

The Lord said to Abram, after Lot had separated from him, "Raise your eyes now, and look from the place where you are, northwards and southwards and eastwards and westwards; for all the land that you see I will give to you and to your offspring for ever. I will make your offspring like the dust of the earth; so that if one can count the dust of the earth, your offspring also can be counted. Rise up, walk through the length and the breadth of the land, for I will give it to you."

So Abram moved his tent, and came and settled by the oaks of Mamre, which are at Hebron; and there he built an altar to the Lord. (Genesis 13:5–18)

Abraham had every right to demand the best land for himself—he was the recipient of the promises; Lot was just along for the ride. Yet Abraham knew that the promises of God would ultimately result in blessings upon his life no matter what his circumstances, so he deferred to Lot. Lot schemed and plotted and picked the more fertile land, despite that it meant living among sinful people who had no regard for the law of the Lord. Abraham trusted not in what his eyes saw, but rather trusted in what the Lord said.

The story goes on to say that Lot eventually needed to be rescued by Abraham (twice!) because of his foolish choices. He had not been able to anticipate the consequences of his actions and fell into a pit dug by his own greed and short-sightedness. Abraham, on the other hand, steadily increased in blessings and influence and went on to see miracles and works of grace in his own life and family. Blessed is the man of meekness. Indeed, he did inherit the land.

King David is another classic Biblical example of meekness. He had been anointed by Samuel as the next king of Israel, but there was one fairly huge problem: Israel already had a king who wasn't interested in retiring. God had rejected Saul as king and David knew it, yet David wouldn't allow his ambition to cause him to strive against the king in order to seize that which was rightfully his. He trusted that the promise of God would eventually come to pass and so he kept himself in a position of obedience and faith.

David had several opportunities to take things into his own hands in order to hasten the day of his prosperity and triumph, but each time he chose the way of meekness. The most famous of these is the time when David was hiding in a cave with several of his men. King Saul, who was hunting for David to have him put to death, went into the cave to relieve himself. He went in to the dark recesses of the cave seeking some privacy, and while he was "doing his thing" David cut off a piece of his royal robe. Saul exited the cave and David followed him out a few minutes later.

> Afterwards David also rose up and went out of the cave and called after Saul, "My lord the king!" When Saul looked behind him, David bowed with his face to the ground, and did obeisance.
>
> David said to Saul, "Why do you listen to the words of those who say, 'David seeks to do you harm'? This very day your eyes have seen how the Lord gave you into my hand in the cave; and some urged me to kill you, but I spared you. I said, 'I will not raise my hand against my lord; for he is the Lord's anointed.' See, my father, see the corner of your cloak in my hand; for by the fact that I cut off the corner of your cloak, and did not kill you, you may know for certain that there is no wrong or treason in my hands. I have not sinned against

you, though you are hunting me to take my life. May the Lord judge between me and you! May the Lord avenge me on you; but my hand shall not be against you. As the ancient proverb says, 'Out of the wicked comes forth wickedness'; but my hand shall not be against you. Against whom has the king of Israel come out? Whom do you pursue? A dead dog? A single flea? May the Lord therefore be judge, and give sentence between me and you. May he see to it, and plead my cause, and vindicate me against you." (1 Samuel 24:8–15)

David chose the path of meekness. He didn't seek his own vindication. He didn't resort to violence or deception to attain prosperity and personal peace; he trusted in the plan of God. He gave himself to mercy and righteousness and believed that God would bless him and establish his house. That is the path of meekness and those who walk it inherit the earth.

But what does meekness look like in twenty-first century North America? This is a dog-eat-dog world, and as Norm Peterson, of *Cheers* fame, once said, "I'm wearing milkbone underwear." Meekness is a difficult virtue to live out in this world, though in fairness it has never been easy and it has never been normal. Living out meekness today requires us to be heaven-focused. There is a way of being heaven-focused that leaves you "of no earthly good," but there is also a way of being heaven-focused that leaves you meek, patient, and even-keeled. That is the way we are searching for.

Fundamentally, I would suggest that meekness grows out of being mournful. There is a sense in which these beatitudes lead into each other, and that is the case here. In becoming mournful, we are losing our love of this world. In becoming meek, we are growing our love for the world in such a way that we remain in this world with a whole different attitude. We are less ambitious, in a worldly sense, and more trusting. We take a longer-term view, we feel less threatened, and we feel more certain.

In terms of how we live out faith, I think a truly saved person manifests meekness in several important ways. I think he still works hard at this job. I think he still has plans, hopes, and ambitions. But I think less of his soul is invested in the outcomes. He wants the promotion, but he won't lie or compromise to get it. He has a financial plan and a desire to retire with some money in the bank, but he won't pass by an opportunity to be generous and he won't downscale his giving in order to experience Freedom 55.

She wants to serve in her church, but she doesn't insist that her gifts be recognised or celebrated. She knows that God will open doors and bless her opportunities. She appreciates the blessings of this life, but she isn't devastated when she loses them, for she knows those losses are temporary. She loves her children, but if one should die before his time she doesn't charge God with wrong, as though she was owed her best life now. She trusts that God knows what he's doing and will one day reveal it. In the meantime, she will delight in him, live to please him, and anticipate the ultimate unfolding of his purpose. That is the life of modern day meekness, and those people still inherit the earth.

Inherit the Earth

We've noticed already that in each of the beatitudes there is a connection made between an aspect of the fully converted life and what might be best called an "eschatological promise." Each aspect of the fully converted life lived *now* is connected to some promise of the end. As with most eschatological promises, there is a sense in which the thing promised will be realized in an ultimate sense after the Second Coming and the Renewal of all things. Simultaneously, there is a sense in which we have the first fruits, the down payment, the initial experience of the thing promised in the here and now. This beatitude promises: *"for they shall inherit the earth."* In what sense is this realized now?

The Bible says again and again that living a righteous life, trusting in the promises instead of grasping and seizing, and crossing the line in order to get ahead do indeed tend to result in greater blessing and earthly prosperity in the present age. Eliphaz the Temmanite, one of Job's counsellors, made this point:

> As I have seen, those who plow iniquity and sow trouble reap the same. (Job 4:8, ESV)

Proverbs 22:8 says:

> Whoever sows injustice will reap calamity (Proverbs 22:8, ESV)

We reap what we sow. There is a rough moral equivalency in the universe. There is a sort of just Providence. There is a moral feedback loop that restrains evil and rewards good. That's all generally true in the here and now. There is a sense in which good people inherit the earth. There is a sense in which living the fully converted life will tend to lead towards prosperity and health.

On the flip side, the Bible seems to imply that if you're a jerk, bad things are going to happen to you. That's true, isn't it? Let's be honest, ninety-five percent of the bad things that happen to us are our own fault. The vast majority of the pain I have suffered in my life has been self-inflicted. All you have to do is go to YouTube and search: "Bad things happening to people" and you will get countless videos of people getting hurt because they are stupid. Usually they are drunk or high or breaking the law. You'll see drunk people falling down or high people jumping off of buildings because they think they can fly or some moron running away from the cops and getting hit by a car as he tries to cross the street; YouTube literally makes its living off the truth of this principle.

Stupid, mean, and evil are generally rewarded with pain and calamity in this life. There is a moral justice to the universe that almost always gets you in the end. Crime don't pay. And conversely, good people living by the Book generally do very well. Study after study says that religious people who generally drink less or not at all, don't smoke, stay married, and obey the laws of the land tend to be healthier, wealthier, and live longer. Obeying God is generally rewarded with increased health, increased prosperity, and length of life on planet earth! Those who meekly trust in the promises of God generally do inherit the earth!

But this eschatological promise is only partially and imperfectly realized in the here and now because of a problem that we talked about in the previous chapter: the devastating and lingering effect of sin and its curse upon all creation. Nature was designed to operate by just moral laws, but nature is groaning under the curse of sin. Paul said that in Romans 8:

> For the creation was subjected to futility, not willingly, but because of Him who subjected it in hope; because the creation itself also will be delivered from the bondage of corruption into the glorious liberty of the children of God. For we know that the whole creation groans and labors with birth pangs together until now. Not only that, but we also who have the firstfruits of the Spirit, even we ourselves groan within ourselves, eagerly waiting for the adoption, the redemption of our body. For we were saved in this hope, but hope that is seen is not hope; for why does one still hope for what he sees? But if we hope for what we do not

see, we eagerly wait for it with perseverance. (Romans 8:20–25, NKJV)

Paul says that the creation is groaning. It's not working the way it was designed because it was subjected to futility, along with all of us, when humanity fell! Sin has entered the created realm like a virus and now the moral software of the universe is a little wonky! Good people don't always live healthy and prosperously and bad people don't always fall into the pit they dug for others. Sometimes bad people get rich, become famous, live fabulously happy lives, and die in their nineties! Sometimes good people are ground into the dust by poverty, disease, and hardship. Sometimes beautiful teenagers, living for Jesus, have car accidents from which they are not miraculously delivered. Why? Because the moral operation of the universe is infected with a virus! But now, because of Christ's victory on the cross, we have the promise that things will be renewed and restored. We *hope in* that, we *expect* that, but we don't have it yet; we have some first fruits, but we are waiting patiently with perseverance in faith for the full consummated reality of those things.

In the end, because God is just, evil will be punished and righteousness will be rewarded. The meek *will* inherit the earth! But—and it's a big but—the end is not yet. This is not the end. Over-realised eschatology is when a person thinks that all of those end-time truths are entirely effective *immediately*.

Let me give you some examples. Is it true that Jesus will heal our bodies and wipe away every tear from our eyes? Yes! But is it true that that will happen *now*? No, not always. That's a truth associated with the *end*. In the meantime, we live in old creation bodies and we groan right along with creation because not everything is working the way it should. That's why in the Bible, when someone is healed, they call it a miracle, not Thursday, because it's *unusual*!

God gives healings as a sign that point to the *end* when he will heal everyone who is in Christ.

We have first fruits in our present experience. Healings are first fruits. They remind us that the full harvest, when it comes, will be really good, so just wait and keep looking forward. In the end, we will all reap what we have sown. Each of us will be judged according to our works. Not that salvation is by works—I'm not saying that—but the Bible is clear that we are all judged, and justice is done. Good is rewarded and evil is punished. You will be healthy and prosperous and *blessed,* child of God. Count on that. But it may not be Thursday; it might be a thousand years from now, but it will come. You may get some first fruits to keep you going, but you may also have to deal with some fallout because it's not the end yet.

That's what makes the prosperity Gospel a heresy. It's not that it isn't true; it's that it leaves out one very important detail: *delay.* They teach that we will inherit the earth *today.* If you aren't inheriting riches on the earth, you must be a sinner! Now, I want to be careful, because I love these brothers and most of what they say is true—God does love us, he does have a wonderful plan for our lives, he does want to bless us and not harm us, he will heal us, he will reward us, he will give us the earth, and we will enjoy his prosperity—but it might not be Thursday. It might be a thousand years from now and we may experience some suffering and hardship and poverty and sickness before we get there.

As preachers and teachers, if we fail to add that detail, we are dangerous and what we say just isn't true enough to be useful. The truth is that we *do* reap what we sow. We *will* inherit the earth… just not always right away, and in large part not until we face Jesus as our judge and comforter. Blessed are the meek, for they shall inherit the earth.

Small Group Discussion

The third beatitude says, *"Blessed are the meek for they shall inherit the earth."* This is supposed to be the way Christians live, and yet nowadays it seems like most Christians are fighting mad about something or other. They are angry about the changes that the pagans are making to "our culture." They are mad as hatters about the immigrants taking our jobs and stealing our opportunities. They hate the government because they can't get their politicians to do what "everyday folks like us want." How is this meekness? What are we left to conclude? That there are Christians who are not meek? Or that such people are not Christians? Regardless of how you feel inclined to answer that question, it is obvious that more teaching on meekness is required in the church. On this issue, we tend to have at least one foot in the ditch of worldliness and if we're not face down in the mud already as a church, we can't be too far away from that reality. So what does it mean to be meek? Let's read the texts below and then address the comprehension task that follows.

    Matthew 5:5
    Psalm 37:1–40
    John 6:15
    Genesis 13:1–11
    Numbers 12:1–13
    1 Samuel 24:1–20
    Philippians 2:5–11
    1 Peter 2:21–23
    Romans 12:19–21
    1 Corinthians 6:1–7
    2 Timothy 2:12
    Luke 14:11

Take a moment and consider the twelve statements below. Circle all that you think correctly reflect the teaching of Jesus on being "meek."

1. A man or woman can never be truly meek if he or she has not first become poor in spirit.
2. If a person has learned what it is to mourn, then he or she is deeply aware that things in the world are not as they ought to be. A meek person frets over that and worries about the present state of affairs.
3. Abraham, Moses, and David were all meek by personality. Some people are born to it. It is not a characteristic for everybody.
4. Meekness is a product and work of the Holy Spirit. No one can achieve true Biblical meekness without the grace and gift of the Holy Spirit.
5. The meek man is keenly sensitive to himself and his rights and will be defensive when accused. He is a just man and does not allow himself to be taken advantage of.
6. The meek woman does not assert her rights, nor does she demand anything for herself. She trusts that the Lord will provide for her needs.
7. The meek man cares only about being justified in the eyes of the Lord. He doesn't need to be publicly vindicated or to sort everything out with those who have wronged him. He would rather be wronged than slow the progress of the Gospel.
8. The meek man knows that no one can harm him. He knows that all he needs and wants will be given him by the Lord at the edge of eternity. Therefore he is at peace, even under trial and even when others take advantage.
9. Meekness means "letting go and letting God." It is the quality of seeking nothing, pursuing nothing, and doing nothing. "Let God sort it out," says the meek person.

10. When a meek person observes injustice or other people suffering abuse, he can have peace knowing that God will take care of them. He is not disturbed, nor does he need to take action.
11. A meek person leaves everything—his rights, his provision, his cause, and his future—in the hands of Almighty God.
12. A meek man doesn't expect to have all of his ambitions in this life realized. Therefore, he is not angry or vengeful or scheming when he finds himself in a disadvantaged situation. He looks to the future and trusts in the promises of God.

Personal Reflection and Evaluation

The Bible says:

> But be doers of the word, and not merely hearers who deceive themselves. For if any are hearers of the word and not doers, they are like those who look at themselves in a mirror; for they look at themselves and, on going away, immediately forget what they were like. But those who look into the perfect law, the law of liberty, and persevere, being not hearers who forget but doers who act— *they will be blessed in their doing*. (James 1:22–25, emphasis mine)

The beatitudes are a description of what *every* Christian should look like. We would be the greatest of fools not to ask a simple follow up question: "To what extent do I look this way? Am I a meek person?"

Take some time to carefully consider the following ten statements. If the statement is *always true of you,* give yourself a score of ten. If it is *sometimes true of you,* give yourself a five. If it is *rarely or never true of you,* give yourself a zero. Tally your score out of a hundred when you have completed the exercise.

1. I am heaven-focused in terms of my worldview. I think a lot about standing before God and that motivates me. I want to hear him say, "Well done thou good and faithful servant." That thought focuses me on a daily basis.
2. I have personal ambitions, goals, and plans, but my soul doesn't rise and fall upon their progress. When I advance, I am pleased, but it doesn't make me feel more or less worthy. When I experience setbacks or failure, I am a little sad, but it doesn't steal my joy or impact my sense of worth in God's eyes in any way.
3. I do not seem to have much of a capacity for nursing anger against people. When people do me wrong, I experience some anger, but it seems to fade very quickly. God will sort it out. I don't feel the need to "speak my piece" or "get my two cents in." God knows my heart and my motives. I am at peace.
4. I like to serve in my area of giftedness in my church, but I don't feel thwarted or disrespected or suppressed if the leadership asks me to serve elsewhere because of a need or because they don't seem to have the same appraisal of my talents as I do. Perhaps the Lord wants me to learn something in these other areas, or perhaps the leaders see the matter more clearly than I do. Either way, I will serve with joy and trust the Lord to open doors in his perfect timing.

5. I love God's Word and desire to learn as much of it as I can. I really do believe that the smartest thing a person could do is read the Bible and bring one's life into perfect alignment with it, by God's grace and with his Spirit, so that God would be pleased and all would be well. I know that doesn't seem like a "wise" strategy for life, but I really believe in it. God's ways are good and lead to my peace and the good of the world!
6. I am interested in world events and enjoy watching the news and knowing what is going on. While I agree that "the world is going to hell in a handbasket," I'm not really alarmed or frightened by it. I know God is in charge and I know his purposes are being worked out. I know his eye is upon me. I will take reasonable precautions against trends in culture, but I won't hoard or panic or fear. His eye is on the sparrow and his eye is on me.
7. In doing my daily business, I enjoy making money and being productive at my tasks and calling. However, I don't ever give in to the pressure to compromise or colour outside the lines in order to get ahead. I don't do jobs for cash under the table, nor do I fail to report income to the taxman. I figure the world will work best if I play by the rules and treat all people fairly and honestly.
8. I am not jealous of those people who get ahead by breaking all the rules. Yes, they drive a nicer car than me, and yes, their garage could conceal a Russian aircraft carrier, but I'm not too concerned about it. I really do believe that God sorts it all out in the end. He will punish those who have abused, defrauded, and lied and he will reward those who have played by the rules and have been kind and generous. Call me naive, but I really trust in that. I am not envious. Rather, I am concerned for the soul of my rich and unsaved neighbour.

9. When I suffer difficulties, disappointments, and personal tragedy, it doesn't make me question God's goodness or power. I don't expect to live my best life now as long as sinful men and women are operating in freedom upon the earth. I do expect that one day the Lord will wipe away every tear, right every wrong, and recompense all those who have suffered under evil and brokenness.
10. When I'm doing well and prospering, I don't feel arrogant or secure. I know it could all be gone tomorrow, so I don't put any trust in it. I try and use my present wealth to bless as many others as I can, knowing that this pleases the Lord. I like to go well above the normal standard of giving when I am able to do so and feel like I am storing up treasure in heaven as I do. What a neat opportunity!

My score out of 100: _____

Evaluated on this date: _____

My prayer of honest response to the Lord:

_____

_____

_____

_____

_____

Chapter Four

Blessed Are Those Who Hunger and Thirst for Righteousness, for They Shall Be Filled

It is often said by scientists that there is about a ninety-five percent similarity (give or take) between the DNA of human beings and that of chimpanzees. This is often used as an argument in support of evolution, in spite of the fact that humans and bananas have a pretty high degree of DNA similarity as well. However, it is not the bizarre conclusions of the biologists that I am drawn to, but rather the high degree of differentiation that is caused by a variant of only five percent. Obviously that five percent is pretty important! I haven't visited any museums built by chimps recently, nor listened to any of their music nor studied in any of their universities. That five percent seems to me to be critically important.

Likewise, a computer programmer knows that, in binary language, having four agreeing digits in a row followed by one digit in disagreement results in a completely different command code.

Little differences make a big deal in the world of computers, in the world of genetics, and also in the world of the Bible. I suppose it is possible that a person might be initially mistaken for a Christian simply because he or she is by personality, temperament, and circumstance some form of "poor in spirit." Perhaps he has had a long string of bad luck that has left him humble and inclined to look for outside support and authority. Perhaps he has had all his illusions shattered by the brutality of this present world. He may, indeed, be one who mourns and has learned at the school of hard knocks that this world is on a path to ruin. He may likewise be meek in the manner of his personal conduct. He may be a bit of a wallflower and a pacifist by personality, and he may even have a bit of the fatalist in him as a residue of some philosophy courses he took in university that he didn't fully understand but that left him with a healthy scepticism about the rat race. At first glance, all this kind of looks like meekness. But here, at Beatitude #4, the lost and the found begin to truly separate. You cannot fake a hunger and a thirst for righteousness. It is not native to human soil; it is planted there by God and the absence of it is proof of his absence.

I recently had coffee with a man who was really struggling. His life had been hit by a tsunami of hurt and loss. The climax of it was the loss of his marriage. He was seething with anger and bitterness and a desire for revenge. He had come to see me because I am a pastor and he had a bit of spiritual heritage and a few bad experiences with therapists and counsellors.

After listening to his story and hearing his desire to press though this for the sake of his son, I asked him a simple question: "Bob (not his real name), would you consider yourself a Christian?"

"Yes," he said. "My parents took me and my sister to church as kids and I made a decision for Christ as a teenager. I haven't been to church in several years and there's a lot in my life that probably shouldn't be there, but yes, I would call myself a Christian."

To which I replied: "Bob, I'm not trying to be offensive, but one thing my years in ministry have taught me is that a ton of people who sincerely think they are Christians are not. Many of them waved their hand at Jesus at youth group once but they didn't know what that meant and they were really just saying that they thought Jesus is good, that he was God's son, and that he died on the cross and rose again and that they wanted to live a blessed life. But except for the blessed life part, that is also the theology of the devil. He was there, he knows all the same things, and he's not a Christian. To be a Christian, according to the Bible, is to be forgiven, *born again by the spirit of God,* and then empowered by his grace to change, day by day, degree by degree into the image of Jesus. So, if you are saved and full of the Spirit, there should be an inner orientation towards the life of righteousness as seen in the life of Jesus Christ. You should have a new 'true north' in your moral compass and a strong desire, almost a maddening instinct, to walk in that direction. Has that ever been true of you?"

Sadly, Bob replied, "No, that has never been true of me. I probably just got caught up in the moment in high school. I do believe in Jesus, but no, I've never felt what you are talking about. That has never characterised my life. I've never really followed Jesus or felt any real compulsion to change."

I shared with Bob that when I was a young man, I remember doing something I knew was wrong. I came home filled with self-loathing and bitter frustration. I literally hammered on my bed with tears in my eyes and cried out to God: "I hate that I've done this! I hate that I've let you down! I hate that my flesh is causing me to make these *stupid* decisions! *Help me!* *Help me* to walk as you walked! I believe that your ways are right and lead to life, but I need your help to walk this way."

I shared how I felt God's grace and help begin to flood my heart over time as I pressed forward in the direction of holiness and Christ-likeness. I asked Bob one more time, for clarity sake, if he had ever felt like that. Had he ever come to the point where he *hated* the sin in his life and *called out longingly* for the grace of the Lord to walk in his way?

"I never have," Bob admitted. "I guess that means that I'm not a real Christian."

You see, this is the five percent difference that makes all the difference in the world. Bob went to church, Bob knew stuff about Jesus, Bob had "orthodox theology," Bob was kind and essentially charitable, but Bob was no more a Christian than that chimpanzee is a bus driver or a classical composer. The difference is in the difference.

King David had the hunger. He prayed:

> As a deer longs for flowing streams, so my soul longs for you, O God. My soul thirsts for God, for the living God. When shall I come and behold the face of God? (Psalm 42:1–2)

The Apostle Paul had it, too:

> *I want to know Christ* and the power of his resurrection and the sharing of his sufferings by becoming like him in his death, if somehow I may attain the resurrection from the dead. Not that I have already obtained this or have already reached the goal; but *I press on* to make it my own, because Christ Jesus has made me his own. Beloved, I do not consider that I have made it my own; but this one thing I do: *forgetting what lies behind and straining forward to what lies ahead*, I press on towards the goal for the prize of the heavenly call of God in Christ Jesus. (Philippians 3:10–14, emphasis mine)

Paul wanted to be *done* with the things of the flesh and he wanted to *press forward* into the things of God. If you have never felt that way, then you're not saved—plain and simple. Does that sound harsh? It's from the Bible. Peter said that we:

> have been chosen and destined by God the Father and sanctified by the Spirit *to be obedient to* Jesus Christ and to be sprinkled with his blood. (1 Peter 1:2, emphasis mine)

He went on to tell his flock:

> Like obedient children, do not be conformed to the desires that you formerly had in ignorance. Instead, as he who called you is holy, be holy yourselves in all your conduct; for it is written, *"You shall be holy, for I am holy."* (1 Peter 1:14–16, emphasis mine)

There is a reason that the Spirit of God is called the Holy Spirit. The Holy Spirit begins to shift and change our moral compass at conversion. He births in us a new orientation towards the character of God. You begin to hate and despise and revile everything in yourself that is opposed to God's character. You hear words come out of your mouth that are arrogant or dishonest or uncharitable or pandering and *you hate those words* before the echo of them leaves the room. You feel a powerful desire welling up inside yourself to be a person of love, justice, truth, kindness, generosity, and faithfulness where before those desires were tempered or not present at all. The Spirit in you leans zealously and jealously towards the God and Creator of your soul. It hates every turn to the right or to the left. That's what it means to hunger and thirst for righteousness and it cannot be faked or mistaken. God meets that hunger with grace and provision and he empowers you to advance along the trajectory of your new orientation. Like wind in your sails, he pushes you in a direction you were once powerless to row in. He will not point you and fail to push you. Those who hunger are filled.

Hungering and thirsting for righteousness isn't really something that you *do* as much as it is something that does you. It consumes you and takes over your heart and your mind. So how do you live that out—or better yet, how do you support that and nurture it? I think the key here is responsiveness and content. I think there are many real Christians who have been told they don't need to pursue righteousness because that is "legalism." There is a special kind of stupid teaching out there in the so-called evangelical world which confuses grace with laziness and self-indulgence. They talk as though if we are saved by grace, we can be lazy and give ourselves permission to do all kinds of stupid things because "it's all grace." These people need to poke themselves in the eye, *hard*, and then read the Book of James. James said:

> What good is it, my brothers and sisters, if you say you have faith but do not have works? Can faith save you? If a brother or sister is naked and lacks daily food, and one of you says to them, "Go in peace; keep warm and eat your fill", and yet you do not supply their bodily needs, what is the good of that? So faith by itself, if it has no works, is dead.
>
> But someone will say, "You have faith and I have works." Show me your faith without works, and I by my works will show you my faith. You believe that God is one; you do well. Even the demons believe—and shudder. Do you want to be shown, you senseless person, that faith without works is barren? Was not our ancestor Abraham

justified by works when he offered his son Isaac on the altar? You see that faith was active along with his works, and faith was brought to completion by the works. Thus the scripture was fulfilled that says, "Abraham believed God, and it was reckoned to him as righteousness", and he was called the friend of God. You see that a person is justified by works and not by faith alone. Likewise, was not Rahab the prostitute also justified by works when she welcomed the messengers and sent them out by another road? For just as the body without the spirit is dead, so faith without works is also dead. (James 2:14–26)

The point James is making is that faith is fulfilled, strengthened, and brought to maturity by exercise and response. Rahab *heard* the story of God's saving works on behalf of the Israelites and she believed those stories were true, but that in itself did not make her a person of faith. It was when she responded to that appropriately that she became a person of faith. That little piece (more than five percent, I should say!) makes all the difference in the world.

Too many Christians have lost their response piece because of bad teaching and lazy learning. They need to become *doers* of the Word, not hearers only deceiving themselves (James 1:22). A Christian who wants to grow in this area needs to make a determined effort to begin hearing again the Word of God with the intention of immediately putting it into practice. If the sermon on Sunday was on forgiveness, go home and write a letter of mercy and release to someone you have been holding a grudge against. Do it that afternoon to strengthen your response muscles.

The second key to living this out is pressing into the content. A ton of Christians nowadays choose to live in near total ignorance of God's Word. The less they know, the less they believe they are responsible for and the less guilty they feel for not living it out. Make the decision to reject that and begin pressing in for more and more content. Read through the Bible in a year, join a group, or download sermons for the drive to work. Lean into and persevere in the content. James talks about that, too:

> But those who look into the perfect law, the law of liberty, and persevere, being not hearers who forget but doers who act—they will be blessed in their doing. (James 1:25)

The word used for "look" there actually means to bend over and peer intently. If you peer *intently* into the word of God and *persevere* and put that into practice, you will be blessed. Blessed are those who hunger and thirst for righteousness, for they shall be filled.

For They Shall Be Filled

Being filled with the Holy Spirit is the climactic promise of the Old Testament. Ezekiel 36 has God promising:

> I will sprinkle clean water on you, and you shall be clean from all your uncleannesses, and from all your idols I will cleanse you. And I will give you a new heart, and *a new spirit I will put within you*. And I will remove the heart of stone from your flesh and give you a heart of flesh. And I will put my Spirit within you, and cause you to walk in my statutes and be careful to obey my rules. You shall dwell in the land that I gave to your fathers, and

you shall be my people, and I will be your God. And *I will deliver you from all your uncleannesses.* (Ezekiel 36:25–29, ESV)

This promise was given while the Jewish people were in exile. The promised land experiment appears to have failed because the people were unable to remain true to God and to their calling. They constantly were falling into compromise with the surrounding peoples and their gods. The temple worship had become so perverted that God completely rejected it. He gave the prophets a vision of his throne literally rolling away from the temple. He wanted it to be absolutely clear: "I am not in what you are doing in my name."

He called on them to repent, but they wouldn't. He sent them prophets, but they refused to listen. And so the inevitable happened. The presence of God left them and they were at the mercy of their enemies and they got trampled. The Babylonians cut through them like a hot knife through butter and defeated the land, destroyed the temple, pulled down the walls of the beautiful city, dispersed the population, and enslaved the nobility. The Jewish dream was over.

Or was it? Jeremiah had spoken about a time in the future when God would renew the covenant, when he would take up again with a remnant of the people and start a new thing. Now, Ezekiel receives a vision in the heart of exile, in the belly of Babylon, that a new day is coming. God will deal with sin, heal the human heart, and once again make his home among mortals. This was the promise. This is what people had been hungering and thirsting for. This was the hunger that Jesus came to satisfy.

The promise said that God would send an emissary to make things right, to deal with sin and to sprinkle us with holy water and make us clean again. And Jesus shedding his blood and giving his life on the cross,

…gave a loud cry and breathed his last. And the curtain of the temple was torn in two, from top to bottom. (Mark 15:37–38)

It was a new day with new hope and the disciples recalled Jesus promising:

> Very truly, I tell you, the one who believes in me will also do the works that I do and, in fact, will do greater works than these, because I am going to the Father. I will do whatever you ask in my name, so that the Father may be glorified in the Son. If in my name you ask me for anything, I will do it. "If you love me, you will keep my commandments. And I will ask the Father, and he will give you another Advocate, to be with you for ever. This is the Spirit of truth, whom the world cannot receive, because it neither sees him nor knows him. You know him, because he abides with you, and he will be in you. I will not leave you orphaned; I am coming to you." (John 14:12–18)

So after the death of Jesus and his resurrection and ascension to the Father, the disciples waited in Jerusalem for the promise of the Spirit.

> When the day of Pentecost had come, they were all together in one place. And suddenly from heaven there came a sound like the rush of a violent wind, and it filled the entire house where they were sitting. Divided tongues, as of fire, appeared among them, and a tongue rested on each of them. All of

them were filled with the Holy Spirit and began to speak in other languages, as the Spirit gave them ability. (Acts 2:1–4)

This is the promise fulfilled! The human heart has been healed and changed and the Spirit of God now abides within! This was the birthday of the church, the new temple of God, and it happened on Pentecost, the day the Jews celebrated the giving of the law to Moses at Mount Sinai. If the first covenant brought the blessing of the law and was celebrated, how much more this renewed covenant with its blessing of the Spirit within to keep the law? The Jews have an oral tradition that's not in the Bible but that was spoken of during the Feast of Pentecost. They taught that the law was given by God in the seventy languages of mankind. Moses heard it in seventy languages but only understood it in Hebrew. They believe God did this to impress upon Moses the universal application of the law and his promises. Now, here in Acts 2, we see that the renewal of the covenant and the fulfilment of the promise that the Spirit would be poured out is accompanied by the sound of many languages. The Spirit, too, is universal in scope and intended for all.

So, how do we get in on that? How can we participate in the promise of the Scripture and the experience of Pentecost? How can we be equipped to do the same and greater works as Jesus? How can we be filled? Does it happen to people when they join the church? When they step forward at a conference? Acts 19:1–6 says:

> While Apollos was in Corinth, Paul passed through the inland regions and came to Ephesus, where he found some disciples. He said to them, "Did you receive the Holy Spirit when you became believers?"

They replied, "No, we have not even heard that there is a Holy Spirit."

Then he said, "Into what then were you baptised?"

They answered, "Into John's baptism."

Paul said, "John baptised with the baptism of repentance, telling the people to believe in the one who was to come after him, that is, in Jesus."

On hearing this, they were baptised in the name of the Lord Jesus. When Paul had laid his hands on them, the Holy Spirit came upon them, and they spoke in tongues and prophesied—altogether there were about twelve of them.

Here we have a story about people who knew something of the Gospel. We really don't know how much they knew; they knew enough that Luke found it convenient to refer to them as "disciples," but it's clear that their faith was in some way deficient. They hadn't even heard that there was a Holy Spirit and they certainly hadn't received the Holy Spirit. Paul completes their understanding, they are baptised in the name of Christ, and they receive the Holy Spirit. They did not receive until they were truly saved.

Why is this important? It's important because throughout the ages there have always been large numbers of people who think they are saved, look a little bit saved, talk a little bit saved, but who show no evidence of the Holy Spirit. When you read the history of the two great awakenings in North America, you discover that these were the very folks that Wesley, Edwards, and Finney preached to. They were not heathens and they were not Buddhists; they were nominal or partial Christians.

Charles G. Finney is often referred to as America's greatest evangelist. In my experience, most evangelical Christians either love him or blame him for most of what is wrong with contemporary evangelism, but whichever side of the conversation you come down on, there's no doubt that God used him as part of American's Second Great Awakening. In his journal, he tells a story of preaching a great fiery sermon on sin and true salvation in a congregational church to people who went there every Sunday and who supposed that they were saved.

> As the people withdrew I observed a woman in one part of the house being supported in the arms of some of her friends, and I went to see what was the matter, supposing that she was in a fainting spell. I soon found that she was not fainting but that she could not speak. There was a look of the greatest anguish in her face and she made me understand that she could not speak. I advised the women to take her home and pray with her to see what the Lord would do. They informed me that she was Miss G—, sister of the well-known missionary, and that she was a member in good standing for several years…
>
> After lying in a speechless state about sixteen hours, Miss G—'s mouth was opened and a new song given to her… She declared that she had been entirely deceived. For eight years she had been a member of the church and thought she was a Christian, but during the sermon the night before she saw that she had never known the true God. When his character arose before her mind as it was then presented her hope perished "like a moth." She said such a view of the holiness of God was presented like a great wave it swept her away from her standing and annihilated her hope in a moment.

I share that story only because it's so typical of the Great Awakenings, and also because it is relevant to our present situation. The truth is, in the New Testament, in the great revivals, and in this present day, the game of the enemy is to remove ingredients from the Gospel, leaving the people deficient in faith. If people truly aren't saved, then they cannot receive the Holy Spirit.

The truly converted person, according to the beatitudes, hungers and thirsts after righteousness and he is filled. In John 14 Jesus said:

Jesus answered him, "Those who love me will keep my word, and my Father will love them, and we will come to them and make our home with them. Whoever does not love me does not keep my words; and the word that you hear is not mine, but is from the Father who sent me." (John 14:23–24)

Jesus said that there was some sort of faith sequence that was birthed in love, was manifest in obedience, and that resulted in empowerment and indwelling. You cannot break the chain and you cannot receive the Holy Spirit if you aren't committed to obedience, if you aren't hungering and thirsting for righteousness. A true believer *hates sin* and *loves righteousness,* and only when God knows that to be true of you will he join himself to you through the Holy Spirit.

Let me add a word, for clarity's sake. I'm not talking about a "second baptism"; that phrase *never appears in the Bible*. I believe that people are filled with the Holy Spirit when they are truly converted, but I also believe in subsequent fillings. There are numerous verses in the Bible that refer to saved people who have the Holy

Spirit receiving subsequent fillings in the Holy Spirit. In Ephesians 5:18, Paul commands his followers:

> Do not get drunk with wine, for that is debauchery; but be filled with the Spirit.

The Greek literally says "be always being filled." Numerous times in Acts, people who have already been baptised in the Holy Spirit are subsequently said to have been filled with the Holy Spirit, and we get this idea that a person can receive fresh filling, or fresh anointing in the Holy Spirit, for specific tasks and can even seek to be "ever being always filled."

I do not believe in "second baptism." The Scriptures don't teach it and experience doesn't require it. I do believe in subsequent experience. I pray that every believer would have a second, third, fourth, fifth, and perpetual experience of the Holy Spirit, each more powerful than the last, but I reject the idea of a two-stage conversion or any notion of two classes of Christians. There are saved people in the church who have and manifest the Holy Spirit and there are deceived people in the church who think they're saved but who aren't. The difference is often located in the fourth beatitude. Blessed are those who hunger and thirst for righteousness, for they shall be filled—here, now, and all the more in the age to come.

Small Group Discussion

The fourth beatitude says, *"Blessed are those who hunger and thirst for righteousness for they shall be filled."* The Bible says that we are, by nature, children of wrath, born with an inclination towards sin, and that when we become Christians we begin to lean towards the way of God in our hearts. Let's read the texts below to reflect further upon that truth and then address the comprehension task that follows.

Matthew 5:6
Psalm 42:1-2
1 Peter 1:1–16
Romans 12:1–21
James 1:22–27
James 2:14–26
2 Corinthians 3:12–18
Philippians 3:7–16
Romans 7:4–25

Take a moment and consider the ten statements below. Circle all that you think correctly reflect the teaching of Jesus on hungering and thirsting for righteousness.

1. Hungering and thirsting for the way of God is a natural human inclination. We are born with a desire to do good and to please the Lord.
2. We are born with a fairly significant skew in our moral compass. The things we are drawn to inevitably result in hurt for ourselves and for those we love and lead down the path to ruin.
3. Part of the grace of God at salvation is a new inward orientation toward the way of God and the Word of God. As I press into that, God showers me with grace, favour, and help to walk in the way of Christ.
4. People who believe in Jesus, who enjoy listening to the Word of God, and who profess to love the Lord and yet feel no inner drive towards repentance and sanctification (becoming holy day by day) cannot be Christians.

5. When people get saved, they are immediately changed into the full likeness of Christ. A truly saved person is an altogether holy person.
6. Sanctification (becoming more and more like Jesus) takes place slowly but surely over time.
7. A real Christian may not be perfect, but he or she is moving consistently in the direction of Christ likeness. They are becoming holy because the Spirit in them is holy and leans zealously in the direction of God.
8. A real Christian *hates* the sin inside themselves and *despises* vehemently the call of the flesh.
9. All this talk about change and zeal and holiness smells a lot like legalism and Pharisaism to me. We are saved by grace and God understands our weakness. If we love Jesus and honestly try to do good, things will work out fine in the end.
10. A real Christian responds to the mercy of God in Jesus Christ by turning her whole life into a response of worship. She begins to put her old self "on the altar" and begins to work with the Spirit to see every aspect of her character transformed.

Personal Reflection and Evaluation

The Bible says:

> But be doers of the word, and not merely hearers who deceive themselves. For if any are hearers of the word and not doers, they are like those who look at themselves in a mirror; for they look at

themselves and, on going away, immediately forget what they were like. But those who look into the perfect law, the law of liberty, and persevere, being not hearers who forget but doers who act—*they will be blessed in their doing.* (James 1:22–25, emphasis mine)

The beatitudes are a description of what *every* Christian should look like. We would be the greatest of fools not to ask a simple follow-up question: "To what extent do I look this way? Am I hungering and thirsting after righteousness?"

Take some time and carefully consider the following ten statements. If the statement is *always true of you,* give yourself a score of ten. If it is *sometimes true of you,* give yourself a five. If it is *rarely or never true of you,* give yourself a zero. Tally your score out of a hundred when you have completed the exercise.

1. I really do desire to live like Christ. I feel an inner compulsion in the direction of holiness that is strong and persistent.
2. I really do *hate* the sin in my life. I'm not perfect and every time I say or do something sinful or arrogant or unloving, *I really hate it.* I am often on my face in tears before the Lord repenting of my sins and seeking help to live in a more Christ-honouring fashion.
3. I really desire to learn as much as I can about the way and Word of God. I read my Bible, listen to messages online, and love going to church to learn about his will.
4. I am not yet what I will be or want to be, but I sense an inner lean forward toward the character of Jesus Christ. I want to be more honest, more truthful, bolder, more

self-giving, more loving, more generous, humbler, kinder, and more thankful.
5. I really do feel like God has changed my heart. There is a huge difference in the leaning of my mind and the inclinations of my heart since I became a Christian.
6. I regularly feel as though God is helping me change and improve. I feel the Holy Spirit flowing into my life, filling me with his presence, and working out fruit and empowered ministry in my life.
7. People have commented on the amount of change in my life over the last several years. They notice a change in my speech, my treatment of others, and my value system and lifestyle.
8. I feel deeply content with the grace of God. I love what God pours into me as I study his Word and reach out to him in prayer. I feel strong and at peace in the Lord.
9. I look back over the last couple of years in my spiritual walk and see a lot of change. I have made several degrees of change by God's grace.
10. I have given God my opinions, habits, and values as an act of worship and invited him to change me into his image by one degree of glory to the next. I love who he is making me to be.

My score out of 100: _____

Evaluated on this date: _____

My prayer of honest response to the Lord:

Chapter Five

Blessed Are the Merciful, for They Shall Obtain Mercy

What does it mean to be merciful? I'm often asked that question by new Christians struggling to get a grip on the lingo. We sometimes use "grace," "love," and "mercy" as synonyms, so it's easy to get confused. The fifth beatitude says, *"Blessed are the merciful,"* not "the gracious" or "the loving," so it's important that we figure out specifically what's being talked about here. As the English word "beatitude" implies, there is an attitude and there is an action. The opposite attitude is best reflected in the story of Jesus' dialogue with some Pharisees in Matthew 12.

> At that time Jesus went through the cornfields on the sabbath; his disciples were hungry, and they began to pluck heads of grain and to eat. When the Pharisees saw it, they said to him, "Look, your

disciples are doing what is not lawful to do on the sabbath."

He said to them, "Have you not read what David did when he and his companions were hungry? He entered the house of God and ate the bread of the Presence, which it was not lawful for him or his companions to eat, but only for the priests. Or have you not read in the law that on the sabbath the priests in the temple break the sabbath and yet are guiltless? I tell you, something greater than the temple is here. But if you had known what this means, 'I desire mercy and not sacrifice', you would not have condemned the guiltless. (Matthew 12:1–7)

These Pharisees delighted in catching people in sin and condemning them before others. They were heresy hunters and finger pointers and they loved it! This is the opposite of the attitude of mercy and Jesus calls them on it. Mercy doesn't delight in finger pointing or heresy hunting. A merciful person has long ago been stripped of those desires as he walked the narrow way. He knows very well the inclination to sin that lived and still struggles within his own heart. He has become convinced that apart from the mercy and grace of God he would have been destroyed by those desires and he's overcome with gratitude that he has been set free by the forgiveness and grace of Almighty God.

Now he looks at his fellow men and women with what might best be described as enlightened pity. He isn't eager to "out" sinners; he's eager to liberate them. He's not a finger pointer; he's a guide to the lost. That's not to say that he isn't a truth teller or that he isn't zealous for the holiness of God's house. We mustn't think that a merciful person is blind to the sin in others or that he simply doesn't care; it's just that he has *compassion* and *pity* for the person who is faltering under their own ignorance and blindness.

The words "mercy" and "compassion" are very much related. In fact, the Greek word that is here translated as "merciful" in Matthew 5:7 can be equally translated as "compassionate." It doesn't mean compassionate in the sense of the charitable impulse. Rather, it means an attitude of understanding pity that makes you want to help people come to the right view of things. Maybe the best positive illustration of this is found in Matthew 9:

> Then Jesus went about all the cities and villages, teaching in their synagogues, and proclaiming the good news of the kingdom, and curing every disease and every sickness. When he saw the crowds, he had compassion for them, because they were harassed and helpless, like sheep without a shepherd. (Matthew 9:35-36)

Do you see the difference in the attitudes of Jesus and the Pharisees? Jesus had compassion on the people he saw who were living lives of bondage and sin and he wanted to help them! He wanted to guide them into life and freedom and salvation! The Pharisees saw people who weren't even doing anything wrong and they leapt at the chance to point fingers and "out" heretics. It never occurred to them to sit patiently with the disciples and discuss ways to honour the Sabbath. Rather, they skipped straight into the condemnation and castigation part that they preferred. A merciful attitude makes you look at a person labouring under sin, sin that may even have resulted in your own hurt and loss, and it makes you want to help them; it makes you want to set them free so that they can enjoy the life they were created to live.

Being merciful, however, is more than just an attitude, though it must first be that; it is also an active response. It's not enough to *feel* merciful towards a lost and labouring person; you have to *act* mercifully. In Matthew 9:35–36, we see the action of mercy paired with the attitude of mercy. Jesus *felt* compassionate and merciful towards them because they were lost and leaderless, so he responded with ministry and instruction. That's one of the primary ways we are to be actively merciful towards lost and labouring people. There is another active form of mercy that the Scripture requires of us and we see that best in the parable of the unmerciful servant.

> Then Peter came and said to him, "Lord, if another member of the church sins against me, how often should I forgive? As many as seven times?"
>
> Jesus said to him, "Not seven times, but, I tell you, seventy-seven times. For this reason the kingdom of heaven may be compared to a king who wished to settle accounts with his slaves. When he began the reckoning, one who owed him ten thousand talents was brought to him; and, as he could not pay, his lord ordered him to be sold, together with his wife and children and all his possessions, and payment to be made. So the slave fell on his knees before him, saying, 'Have patience with me, and I will pay you everything.' And out of pity for him, the lord of that slave released him and forgave him the debt. But that same slave, as he went out, came upon one of his fellow-slaves who owed him a hundred denarii; and seizing him by the throat, he said, 'Pay what you owe.' Then his fellow-slave fell down and pleaded with him, 'Have patience with me, and I will pay you.' But he refused; then he went and threw him into prison until he should

pay the debt. When his fellow-slaves saw what had happened, they were greatly distressed, and they went and reported to their lord all that had taken place. Then his lord summoned him and said to him, 'You wicked slave! I forgave you all that debt because you pleaded with me. *Should you not have had mercy on your fellow-slave, as I had mercy on you?*' And in anger his lord handed him over to be tortured until he should pay his entire debt. So my heavenly Father will also do to every one of you, if you do not forgive your brother or sister from your heart." (Matthew 18:21–35, emphasis mine)

When fellow Christians who are struggling with their own sin wound and injure us, as surely they will within the church, our attitude of mercy must result in the *action* of merciful release. We must not hold onto moral debts. We must keep no record of wrongs. We must not make people pay, or God will make us pay.

If I may step way out on a limb here, this teaching needs to find its way into many so-called Christian marriages. Christian wives and husbands are every bit as good as their pagan counterparts at making their spouses pay dearly for their transgressions. Wives withhold sex while husbands withhold affection and communication. According to Jesus, persisting in this unmerciful activity becomes proof that you are unsaved and uncovered by the blood of his sacrifice. Those who cannot release their fellow Christians from moral debt give convincing proof that they have never apprehended and applied with grateful faith the offer of forgiveness and mercy that is given in Jesus Christ. Those people pay their own debts. Failure to act mercifully condemns us as unforgiven people. Blessed are the merciful, for they shall obtain mercy.

In terms of living out mercy in an active sense, Christians are required to engage with lost and labouring people at the point of sin and failure. Again, being merciful doesn't mean you don't engage with people over sin. You do; you just do it with a totally different attitude than a fault finder and heresy hunter. Jesus laid out a process for engaging with fellow Christians over sin:

> If another member of the church sins against you, go and point out the fault when the two of you are alone. If the member listens to you, you have regained that one. But if you are not listened to, take one or two others along with you, so that every word may be confirmed by the evidence of two or three witnesses. If the member refuses to listen to them, tell it to the church; and if the offender refuses to listen even to the church, let such a one be to you as a Gentile and a tax-collector. (Matthew 18:15–17)

A lot of people hear that and think to themselves, *So, if a person refuses to be corrected even by the church, I am to treat them like a Gentile and a tax collector. Great! I can spit at them, hiss at them, and treat them like dogs!* But is that how Jesus treated Gentiles and tax collectors? No! Those were the very people he came to with the message of mercy and salvation. Jesus isn't telling us to mistreat folks like that; he's saying that they obviously aren't saved and need the Gospel!

A real Christian would have responded to gentle instruction long ago. Only a non-Christian with an unconverted heart would persevere so long in hurtful and sinful behaviour. Jesus, the very person who requires us to be merciful, also requires us to engage with fellow Christians over the sin binding them with the end that they will be led deeper into the life of faith and freedom. If they don't respond, it's because they're not walking in faith and freedom and we need to then evangelise them. Being merciful in an active sense requires us to lovingly lead people away from sin and into life.

Paul taught this clearly to the Galatians:

> My friends, if anyone is detected in a transgression, you who have received the Spirit should restore such a one in a spirit of gentleness. Take care that you yourselves are not tempted. Bear one another's burdens, and in this way you will fulfil the law of Christ. (Galatians 6:1–2)

James, the brother of Jesus, thought this was so important that he offered this charge as the conclusion to the letter he sent out to all his churches:

> My brothers and sisters, if anyone among you wanders from the truth and is brought back by another, you should know that whoever brings back a sinner from wandering will save the sinner's soul from death and will cover a multitude of sins. (James 5:19–20)

If you want to live as a merciful person, you have to engage with lost and labouring people in order to set them free and point them in the way of life. You have to do this not as a heresy hunter, not by blogging about how sinful most Christians are, not by having an indexed website that points out the flaws of every Christian who has ever tried to teach or lead, but rather by patiently bearing with people and coaching them back to the ways that lead to life.

They Shall Obtain Mercy

This is where I'm supposed to switch from describing mercy to explaining the blessing that is associated with it, both in the present and in the life to come. This time, I want to do that in kind of a sneaky way. I want to first unpack the archetypal story about mercy in the New Testament and then turn that around and say, "This is how God will bless you." There is a reason for this approach, which I will explain at the end.

The archetypal story about mercy was, as you would expect, told by Jesus. He was a very good storyteller. The context or cause for the story was a question from an eager young man. The young man wants to be a disciple of Jesus and Jesus deals with him fairly on that basis. Now, is the young man arrogant? Of course, all young men are arrogant. Later the text says he wants to justify himself. Every young student wants to justify himself. I see myself in this young man. This is me. He is sitting in the front row with his pre-highlighted textbooks, eager to show the Rabbi that he is ready to go and eager to learn, halfway down the road Jesus is taking him. "I'm already tracking with you, Professor. I've written the notes for your next class." This is me ten years ago. I like this guy, so be nice to him.

> And behold, a lawyer stood up to put him to the test, saying, "Teacher, what shall I do to inherit eternal life?"
>
> He said to him, "What is written in the Law? How do you read it?"
>
> And he answered, "You shall love the Lord your God with all your heart and with all your soul and with all your strength and with all your mind, and your neighbor as yourself."

And he said to him, "You have answered correctly; do this, and you will live."

But he, desiring to justify himself, said to Jesus, "And who is my neighbor?"

Jesus replied, "A man was going down from Jerusalem to Jericho, and he fell among robbers, who stripped him and beat him and departed, leaving him half dead. Now by chance a priest was going down that road, and when he saw him he passed by on the other side. So likewise a Levite, when he came to the place and saw him, passed by on the other side. But a Samaritan, as he journeyed, came to where he was, and when he saw him, he had compassion. He went to him and bound up his wounds, pouring on oil and wine. Then he set him on his own animal and brought him to an inn and took care of him. And the next day he took out two denarii and gave them to the innkeeper, saying, 'Take care of him, and whatever more you spend, I will repay you when I come back.' Which of these three, do you think, proved to be a neighbor to the man who fell among the robbers?"

He said, "The one who showed him mercy."

And Jesus said to him, "You go, and do likewise." (Luke 10:25–37, ESV)

Before we explain this story, I need to clarify a few words. Some people get confused because this passage starts off talking about love and ends up talking about mercy. The summary verse at the end confuses some:

> "Which of these three, do you think, proved to be a neighbor to the man who fell among the robbers?"
> He said, "The one who showed him mercy."
> And Jesus said to him, "You go, and do likewise." (Luke 10:36–37, ESV)

Is this a passage about love or mercy? In both the Hebrew and Greek languages, love and mercy are overlapping concepts. The Hebrew word for mercy is *hesed* and some of your Bibles translate that as mercy and some as steadfast love. The Greek word for mercy is *elios*, which is translated variously as mercy, compassion, or love. Think of mercy as a type of love. It's a love for your fellow man that is active and quick to respond to brokenness or need. Does that help? Okay, let's dive into the meaning of this story before turning the tables and talking about how God blesses us this way.

After some back and forth about the definition of salvation from the Old Testament, which both Jesus and the young man agree upon—salvation being understood as restoration to a loving relationship with God that overflows into right relationship with one's neighbour—the young man asks for a picture of that standard. "Show me what loving the neighbour looks like." Jesus actually had to help the young man to that place. His original question was more like: "Whom shall I love?" and Jesus improved on that, saying rather, "Let's talk about *how* we shall love."

The young man eagerly listens to Jesus as he paints a picture of kingdom love and mercy. Scholars agree that the story we're looking at is a picture of the saved man. It's a picture of perfect love, merciful love towards one's neighbour. Jesus is saying, "If you want to follow me down the path of salvation, down the narrow way, you will need to walk like this." So let's look. How does a fully converted person love and show mercy? How does he need to conduct him or herself in this world?

First of all, a kingdom man, a saved man, walks with eyes wide open to the needs and hurts of those around him. Jesus walked this way.

> When *he saw the crowds*, he had compassion for them, because they were harassed and helpless, like sheep without a shepherd. (Matthew 9:36, emphasis mine)

The Good Samaritan walked this way as well:

> *When he saw him*, he was moved with pity. (Luke 10:33)

The kind of love that characterises the eternal kingdom of God is not a love that hides itself from the reality of the world. It's so easy to do that, so easy to turn the channel when the World Vision commercial comes on, so easy to look straight ahead when you drive through parts of town, so easy to live in your tidy neighbourhood and hide in your hermetically sealed car as you drive through a dying world. It's so easy to put our kids in private school, so easy to withdraw, so easy to isolate for fear of contamination. Don't do it. We need to see if we would be merciful.

We also need to be prepared to stop. Surprisingly, the characters in this story who provide the contrast to the way of the kingdom are a priest and a Levite. They are the ones a Jewish audience would normally assume were walking the narrow way, but Jesus says they aren't. Maybe they're too busy to see and too busy to stop. Maybe they're concerned with other things. Priests and Levites oversaw the worship of the temple, and if they had contact with a dead body they would be ceremonially unclean and unable to serve. These were men who thought that the heart of the law was purity and that God preferred worship to mercy. The young lawyer would have recognised this rebuke and agreed with it because the Bible says:

> For I desire mercy and not sacrifice, And the knowledge of God more than burnt offerings. (Hosea 6:6, NKJV)

To know God is to know what matters most to him. This verse says that the goal of God, his first priority, is to restore people to a right knowledge of him that overflows into a right relationship with fellow man. Everything else is mean and method. Converted people get that. Kingdom people make time for that. They won't get caught up or distracted by other things. They stop and seek to know the Lord, and they stop and seek to love their fellow man. If you don't have time, you're not walking the way.

And as you walk this way, you need to be willing to get involved. Christianity, the way of the kingdom, is not a way of words, sentiment, or even mere belief. It's a way of active engagement with God and with our fellow man. Evangelicals need to hear this. We think we are saved because we have belief and sentiment. We believe in Jesus and our hearts hurt for poor people. That doesn't cut it.

> What good is it, my brothers and sisters, if you say you have faith but do not have works? Can faith save you? If a brother or sister is naked and lacks daily food, and one of you says to them, "Go in peace; keep warm and eat your fill", and yet you do not supply their bodily needs, what is the good of that? So faith by itself, if it has no works, is dead. (James 2:14–17)

The Good Samaritan got involved! He didn't weep over the man and he didn't pray for him; he picked him up, bandaged his wounds, poured wine on them as a disinfectant, oil to speed healing and to sooth, and then he took him to an inn and set him up with ongoing care. That's serious involvement! And broad involvement. One of the surprising things about this story, for the young man who was hearing it, was the ethnic breadth of it. He would have agreed that a Jew must treat his neighbour Jew this way; there was nothing new in that. Deuteronomy 15 says that much:

> If there is among you anyone in need, a member of your community in any of your towns within the land that the Lord your God is giving you, do not be hard-hearted or tight-fisted towards your needy neighbour. You should rather open your hand, willingly lending enough to meet the need, whatever it may be. Be careful that you do not entertain a mean thought, thinking, "The seventh year, the year of remission, is near", and therefore view your needy neighbour with hostility and give nothing; your neighbour might cry to the Lord against you, and you would incur guilt. Give liberally and be ungrudging when you do so, for on this account the Lord your God will bless you in all your work and in all that you undertake. Since there will never cease to be some in need on the earth, I therefore command you, "Open your hand to the poor and needy neighbour in your land." (Deuteronomy 15:7–11)

What's surprising is that this standard is to be applied, according to Rabbi Jesus, across ethnic boundaries. Jesus says that a saved man, a truly converted man—a kingdom man—loves everyone this way; he loves broadly, extravagantly, and with uncommon mercy. That's why mercy is such a useful word. Love means too many things and far too little to too many people. Mercy is a bit more specific and convicting.

And finally, as you walk this kingdom way, you will learn to hold your possessions very loosely. The kingdom of God is about eternal things. God, truth, love, mercy, justice—*people*. It's not about money or stuff, so people on this path can take them or lose them. The Apostle Paul was that guy:

> Not that I am referring to being in need; for I have learned to be content with whatever I have I know what it is to have little, and I know what it is to have plenty. In any and all circumstances I have learned the secret of being well-fed and of going hungry, of having plenty and of being in need. (Philippians 4:11–12)

Paul says, "Not that I prefer poverty. If I get to choose between eating and not eating, I'll chose eating, but whatever comes my way is fine. I'm in this for the kingdom, not for the money." Christians don't need to despise money; we just need to part with it easily. The Bible says that the Samaritan gave the innkeeper two denaraii, which according to historical records would have purchased the man two months' stay and board. Two months' stay and board… that's like $2500 in today's terms and he said that, if costs rose above that, to put it on his tab. Who does that for a complete stranger? The one who loves with kingdom love. The converted man of mercy.

This is what it looks like for a person restored to a loving relationship with God to walk in merciful love towards his neighbour, Jesus says. This is the narrow way.

I didn't invent the connection between this story and the fifth beatitude. Scholars often point out that the Good Samaritan story is really just the narrative version of the propositional statement:

> Blessed are the merciful, for they shall receive mercy. (Matthew 5:7, ESV)

It doesn't take a degree in Biblical Studies to notice that receiving mercy is in some way connected to extending it. If we deny that, we have to seriously edit the entire Bible. So what is the relationship?

Merciful living is not the means of salvation; it is the *standard* of salvation. This is the path that saved men and women walk on and any honest person falls on their face when they see it. Only a truly converted person, filled with the Holy Spirit, can begin to walk this way in the here and now of planet earth. This is the way of mercy, and it is only walked by grace.

I began this section by promising that I would explain in what sense those who extend mercy will receive it and I promised I would explain why I took this roundabout way of getting to it. Well, here it is. The early church actually taught that Jesus was the Good Samaritan. He was painting a picture of his own walk and ministry. He is the one who finds us half-dead in our sins, lying rejected on the side of the road. He takes pity on us, binds our wounds, pours the wine of his blood and the oil of his spirit upon us, and puts us in a safe place (the church), promising to return to ensure our full health. That is the mercy we receive in this present life.

Jesus is our Good Samaritan. He sees us trapped in our sins. He sees us lying in the ditch beside the road we can no longer walk on. He sees us beaten and abused by our enemy and he takes pity on us. He stops. He gets involved and he pays the price. He begins to heal us, restore us, and renew us right here, right now, and he completes that work of mercy at the renewal of all things. Like the rest of this fallen world, we long for that day:

> Then I saw a new heaven and a new earth, for the first heaven and the first earth had passed away, and the sea was no more. And I saw the holy city, new Jerusalem, coming down out of heaven from God, prepared as a bride adorned for her husband.
> And I heard a loud voice from the throne saying, "Behold, the dwelling place of God is with man. He will dwell with them, and they will be his people, and God himself will be with them as their God. He will wipe away every tear from their eyes, and death shall be no more, neither shall there be mourning nor crying nor pain anymore, for the former things have passed away."
> And he who was seated on the throne said, "Behold, I am making all things new." Also he said, "Write this down, for these words are trustworthy and true." And he said to me, "It is done! I am the Alpha and the Omega, the beginning and the end. To the thirsty I will give from the spring of the water of life without payment. The one who conquers will have this heritage, and I will be his God and he will be my son." (Revelation 21:1–7, ESV)

The Good Samaritan mercy of Jesus is a blessing beyond compare in this present life; in the life to come, it is literally out of this world. Blessed are the merciful, for they shall obtain mercy.

Small Group Discussion

The fifth beatitude says, *"Blessed are the merciful for they shall obtain mercy."* This is an attitude and active orientation born out of profound gratitude for the mercy we have experienced at the cross of Jesus Christ. We are forgiven people who have been found out of utter lostness and led into abundant life. As such, we want to lead others and see them released from all their labouring and bondage. That's what it means to be merciful and these are the ones who obtain mercy. Let's read the texts below to reflect upon these concepts and then address the comprehension task that follows.

> Matthew 5:7
> Matthew 6:14–15
> Matthew 18:23–35
> Luke 10:25–37
> Luke 23:34
> Psalm 66:18

Take a moment and consider the ten statements below. Circle all that you think correctly reflect the teaching of Jesus on being merciful.

1. Only a man who knows there is no righteousness within himself and who has thrown himself upon the mercy of Almighty God will be able to show mercy with cheerfulness to others.
2. Being merciful means having a relaxed attitude towards sin. Don't stress about it in yourselves or in other believers. A merciful person always shows grace towards sinners.

3. Being merciful means that you can easily forgive the wrongs done to you. It doesn't mean that you condone or fail to correct sin in yourself or in others.
4. Our definition of mercy has to be based in the nature of God. God takes sin very seriously; he sacrificed his son to pay for it and will send many people to hell if they haven't apprehended by faith that sacrifice. God is also capable of extending forgiveness to those who have wronged him. Our definition of mercy must balance those facts.
5. If I have truly become convinced of my own utter sinfulness and wretchedness, and if I have truly hungered and thirsted for righteousness from God, and if I have received that very thing I sought for, I will now look on other men and women differently. I will pity them and view them as captives to a thing from which I have been liberated and wish only to see them free as I am. If I do not look at them that way; it is proof that I myself have not travelled to this point on the narrow way.
6. A person who is not merciful is not saved.
7. If I show mercy to others, if I grant forgiveness to others, I shall be saved.
8. People who get easily offended, carry long grudges, and are callous to the needs of broken people give evidence that they are not saved. They have obviously neither mourned over their own brokenness nor rejoiced over the provision of an undeserved righteousness. They have no poverty of spirit and therefore have never passed through the narrow gate.
9. If I'm not merciful, there is only one explanation: I have never understood the grace and mercy of God, I am outside Christ, I am yet in my sins, and I am unsaved.

10. This beatitude reminds a person that being a Christian isn't simply a matter of one's attitude and status with God; it also involves our attitude and status with other people.

Personal Reflection and Evaluation:

The Bible says:

> But be doers of the word, and not merely hearers who deceive themselves. For if any are hearers of the word and not doers, they are like those who look at themselves in a mirror; for they look at themselves and, on going away, immediately forget what they were like. But those who look into the perfect law, the law of liberty, and persevere, being not hearers who forget but doers who act— *they will be blessed in their doing.* (James 1:22–25, emphasis mine)

The beatitudes are a description of what *every* Christian should look like. We would be the greatest of fools not to ask a simple follow up question: "To what extent do I look this way? Am I an actively merciful person?"

Take some time and carefully consider the following ten statements. If the statement is *always true of you,* give yourself a score of ten. If it is *sometimes true of you,* give yourself a five. If it is *rarely or never true of you,* give yourself a zero. Tally your score out of a hundred when you have completed the exercise.

1. I carry a deep awareness within me that I have been forgiven much. Like God told the Israelites, "Remember the

long road by which you have come." I am a super sinner, a worthless wretch, and deserve nothing but exile from the Presence of a holy, just, righteous God. I live in that awareness and am full of gratitude and humility for the mercy God has shown me.
2. I am able to forgive people and overlook wrongs done to me with relative ease. I do not stew long or hard over slights and injuries, real or imagined. I believe the best and extend generous amounts of mercy to the people I share space with, particularly in the church.
3. I neither require closure, nor do I need to be heard or understood, in order to move on. Whenever I can do so without endangering other potential victims, I prefer to just let it go, preferring to be wronged than to slow the cause of the Gospel or waste time assigning ratio of blame.
4. Because I was rescued out of a deep and destructive bondage, I have great sympathy for people who have yet to be set free. I hate addiction, I hate vice, I hate confusion, I hate deception, I hate ignorance, and I hate the one who engineers these things in the lives of people God created to be his sons and daughters. I desperately want to see people set free from that garbage so that they can live free and live well under God's design and care.
5. I think a lot about the blessings of eternity that have been given me freely and undeservedly by the mercy of Jesus. As a result, I find that injustices in the here and now don't greatly impact me. These are momentary afflictions, unworthy of comparison to the blessings near at hand.
6. I am at peace. I am not embroiled in conflicts with people. Not everyone likes me, but I am not at war with anyone. I wish well for all.
7. I am not a passive observer of the world, as though I already lived someplace else. I use my time here to bless and

serve others. I am outraged by the hurt, abuse, corruption, and abuse I see in this world because of the corrosive influence of sin and diligently strive against it by God's grace and power. I am impacted by the suffering I see in others and determined to help others.

8. When I go to the Lord in prayer, if I perceive unforgiveness or bitterness in my own heart, I immediately move to address it. I understand that as a forgiven and restored person, I need to be at peace, so far as it depends on me, with other people.
9. I am actively engaged in a gentle way with Christians who are wrestling with sin. I engage that in humility and in determination to see my brother or sister free by the grace and help of God. I do not turn away from my brother's bondage to sin and darkness.
10. I keep very short accounts. I extend forgiveness and release to brothers and sisters who wrong me. I am living free and loving it!

My score out of 100: _____

Evaluated on this date: _____

MY PRAYER OF HONEST RESPONSE TO THE LORD:

_____

_____

_____

_____

Chapter Six

Blessed Are the Pure in Heart, for They Shall See God

The Bible generally doesn't have a lot of good things to say about the state of the human heart.

> The heart is deceitful above all things, And desperately wicked; Who can know it? (Jeremiah 17:9, NKJV)

This has been the assessment of God upon the heart of mankind for a very long time, the Bible says in Genesis:

> The Lord saw that the wickedness of man was great in the earth, and that every intention of the thoughts of his heart was only evil continually. (Genesis 6:5, ESV)

In the Bible, the heart is understood as the centre of a person's identity and being. It is the place where values are held, where thoughts are born, and where speech originates, for good or evil. Jesus said:

> The good person out of the good treasure of his heart produces good, and the evil person out of his evil treasure produces evil, for out of the abundance of the heart his mouth speaks. (Luke 6:45, ESV)

The human heart is a wellspring which can produce good or evil depending entirely on what we place at its centre. Something will be at the centre of our hearts to determine the outcome of our lives. So what are the options? The Bible suggests that all blessed life begins with putting God at the centre of one's love, allegiance, and attention. Jesus taught that this was where it all began. When asked what the greatest commandment was, he replied without hesitation by quoting from Deuteronomy 6:

> You shall love the Lord your God with all your heart and with all your soul and with all your might. (Deuteronomy 6:5, ESV)

If God is at the centre of your heart, then the produce of your life, speech, and conduct will be good. If anything else occupies that place, the produce of your life will be some flavour of poison. That's why the Bible seems to be so agitated about the issue of idolatry. Idolatry simply means having anything else at the centre of your heart. If anything else fills the space that was created for God alone, you have an idol problem and that problem will work its way out into every corner and facet of your life.

Being pure in heart means being singular in your devotion to God. It means that God doesn't share the throne of your life with anything or anyone else. It means that when decisions are made, there is only one true north on your compass, only one Shepherd and only one Captain. Being pure in heart means that you are a one-God man or a one-Lord lady. In that sense, being pure in heart has obvious parallels with being faithful in love and marriage.

The Bible frequently uses adultery as a metaphor for idolatry, sometimes in a way that is almost alarming to the modern-day reader. Consider, for example, Ezekiel 16, where God addresses his people as a husband might address a wife who has strayed:

> Adulterous wife, who receives strangers instead of her husband! Men give gifts to all prostitutes, but you gave your gifts to all your lovers, bribing them to come to you from every side with your whorings So you were different from other women in your whorings. No one solicited you to play the whore, and you gave payment, while no payment was given to you; therefore you were different Therefore, O prostitute, hear the word of the Lord: Thus says the Lord God, Because your lust was poured out and your nakedness uncovered in your whorings with your lovers, and with all your abominable idols, and because of the blood of your children that you gave to them, therefore, behold, I will gather all your lovers with whom you took pleasure, all those you loved and all those you hated. I will gather them against you from every side and will uncover your nakedness to them, that they may see all your nakedness. And I will judge you as women who commit adultery and shed blood are judged, and bring upon you the blood of wrath

and jealousy. And I will give you into their hands, and they shall throw down your vaulted chamber and break down your lofty places. They shall strip you of your clothes and take your beautiful jewels and leave you naked and bare. They shall bring up a crowd against you, and they shall stone you and cut you to pieces with their swords. And they shall burn your houses and execute judgments upon you in the sight of many women. I will make you stop playing the whore, and you shall also give payment no more. So will I satisfy my wrath on you, and my jealousy shall depart from you. I will be calm and will no more be angry. (Ezekiel 16:22–42, ESV)

God charges Israel with preferring other gods to him. They haven't rejected God, but they also enjoy worshipping the gods of the people around them. They want an open marriage! They would still worship God and go to temple, but why be so exclusive? Why tie yourself down to a single allegiance? Why not take a balanced approach to spirituality? One doesn't want to be a fanatic, after all. But God is a jealous God and demands *wholehearted* allegiance and devotion. God will be at the centre or God will make war from outside. He will not share space.

It isn't just other religions that God is opposed to; it's also other human allegiances. In Jeremiah, we see God using the same language to condemn a political alliance. The people of God had sought protection from the Egyptians instead of trusting in God alone. Not only did they look to Egypt to supply something that God said he would provide, but now as a vassal state they found themselves having potentially contrary allegiances. God rebuked them, saying:

> And now what do you gain by going to Egypt to drink the waters of the Nile? Or what do you gain by going to Assyria to drink the waters of the Euphrates? Your evil will chastise you, and your apostasy will reprove you. Know and see that it is evil and bitter for you to forsake the Lord your God; the fear of me is not in you, declares the Lord God of hosts. For long ago I broke your yoke and burst your bonds; but you said, "I will not serve." Yes, on every high hill and under every green tree you bowed down like a whore. (Jeremiah 2:18–20, ESV)

God is opposed to any other loyalty occupying the space in your heart he has reserved for himself. Obviously that outlaws other religions, it outlaws human allegiances that compete for our obedience and trust, and it outlaws excessive pursuit of material gain and physical pleasure. In the Bible, "lust" is spoken of as idolatry:

> Put to death therefore what is earthly in you: sexual immorality, impurity, passion, evil desire, and covetousness, which is idolatry. (Colossians 3:5, ESV)

A lust can become a sort of "mini-god" in our lives. It can dictate our behaviours, compete for our time, and consume our attention. Much of what we call "addiction" today could rightly be labelled "idolatry." Is sex a sin? No, of course not. If you are enjoying human sexuality within the boundaries God provided, then it's a blessing. But if the pursuit of sexual pleasure takes you outside the boundaries God has set and it begins to alter your behaviour, dominate your thoughts, and determine your movements and objectives, then it has become an addiction and an idol. It sits in the centre and God will not be roommates with your lust.

The pursuit of wealth is just as addictive and idolatrous as the pursuit of sexual pleasure. It begins to influence our morality, determine our movements, and eat up our thought life and focus. Is it wrong to work hard and make money? No, of course not. But if the pursuit of wealth and possession takes you outside God's moral boundaries and begins to dominate your thoughts, your decision making, and your movements, it has become an addiction and an idol. It sits in the centre and God will not share space with Mammon.[4] Jesus said:

> No one can serve two masters; for either he will hate the one and love the other, or else he will be loyal to the one and despise the other. You cannot serve God and mammon. (Matthew 6:24, NKJV)

Having a pure heart, therefore, is like being a husband who has no girlfriends on the side. It's like being a wife who doesn't have to chat with strangers on the internet. She looks to her husband to provide all that she needs. He looks to his wife as the object of his love and attention. You don't want a third party in your marriage and you cannot have a third party in your worship. Being pure of heart means that your compass has only one true north and there are no other magnets in your life messing up your sense of direction. Those people find God. This has been the promise of the Bible from the start. Moses told his people that if they ever found themselves scattered into foreign lands because of their idolatries, they needed only to repent, cast off their idols, and purify their allegiances to find him again:

---

4 "Mammon" was the Chaldean god of money and became a common way of describing the love of money when it has become idolatrous. We might say, "Worshipping the almighty dollar." Same idea.

> But from there you will seek the Lord your God and you will find him, if you search after him with all your heart and with all your soul. (Deuteronomy 4:29, ESV)

The Bible says that even when you live in a land of idols, if you keep them outside of you and let nothing in, the compass of your heart will lead you straight back to God and you will find him. Blessed are the pure in heart, for they shall see God.

Practically speaking, how do we become increasingly pure in heart? As we continue to work out our salvation, how do we press deeper into this aspect of the fully converted life? Perhaps the best way to approach it is to carry on with the analogy of becoming a more faithful and devoted husband or wife. The Bible suggests this line of thinking, so it must be acceptable and profitable. How then could you become a more devoted and loyal husband? First of all, I would suggest that you not allow yourself to receive anything from a woman that you should receive from your wife. There is a type of emotional, physical, and sexual support that one receives from one's wife that can *never* be received from another woman. Jesus, in Matthew 5, says that this begins with the eye. You cannot even look with lust upon another woman. You need to be devoted to your wife in eye, mind, hand, and body. You need to be focused on giving to her what it is your duty and responsibility to give. You need to guard yourself from other attractions. In Proverbs, the wise old father gives his son some excellent advice:

> For at the window of my house I have looked out through my lattice, and I have seen among the simple, I have perceived among the youths, a young man lacking sense, passing along the street near her corner, taking the road to her house in the

twilight, in the evening, at the time of night and darkness. And behold, the woman meets him, dressed as a prostitute, wily of heart.

She is loud and wayward; her feet do not stay at home; now in the street, now in the market, and at every corner she lies in wait. She seizes him and kisses him, and with bold face she says to him, "I had to offer sacrifices, and today I have paid my vows; so now I have come out to meet you, to seek you eagerly, and I have found you. I have spread my couch with coverings, colored linens from Egyptian linen; I have perfumed my bed with myrrh, aloes, and cinnamon. Come, let us take our fill of love till morning; let us delight ourselves with love. For my husband is not at home; he has gone on a long journey; he took a bag of money with him; at full moon he will come home."

With much seductive speech she persuades him; with her smooth talk she compels him. All at once he follows her, as an ox goes to the slaughter, or as a stag is caught fast till an arrow pierces its liver; as a bird rushes into a snare; he does not know that it will cost him his life. And now, O sons, listen to me, and be attentive to the words of my mouth. *Let not your heart turn aside to her ways; do not stray into her paths,* for many a victim has she laid low, and all her slain are a mighty throng. Her house is the way to Sheol, going down to the chambers of death. (Proverbs 7:6–27, ESV, emphasis mine)

A good husband doesn't even walk down the street of a loose woman. He doesn't expose himself to her seductions because he knows the weakness of his own flesh. This is not defeatism or lack of faith; this is *wisdom!* The Apostle Paul said to young men under his teaching:

> *Flee also youthful lusts*; but pursue righteousness, faith, love, peace with those who call on the Lord out of a pure heart. (2 Timothy 2:22, NKJV, emphasis mine)

Flee youthful lusts! Run away! Guard your heart and your devotion. That is good advice for any young husband—or any young wife, for that matter.

The same principles apply to being a fully devoted follower of Jesus Christ. You need to guard yourself against other influences. Watch how much media you consume. Media is the song of the whore of Babylon. That's not to say that everything on TV is propaganda for the devil, but make no mistake, the devil whispers in the media. The whore sings her siren song on all the airwaves. She wants her voice in your heart when decisions are being made. Shut her out by turning her off. Flee. Turn it off. Read good books. Choose which streets you allow your mind to go down.

You must also not allow yourself to receive something from something or someone that you were meant to receive from God. For example, do not take comfort or security from your money. Do not take identity or affirmation from your wealth. The Bible warns against this:

> As for the rich in this present age, charge them not to be haughty, nor to set their hopes on the uncertainty of riches, but on God, who richly provides us with everything to enjoy. (1 Timothy 6:17, ESV)

It is not a sin to have riches, but it is idolatry to trust in them. It is idolatry to gain your identity from them. Security and identity are to come from God.

You must also make sure that you give to God the things you are supposed to give him. As a husband must give his affection and provision to his wife, so a Christian must give his worship and his service to God. When you spend your tithe on a family vacation or a big screen TV, you are doing the same thing as if a husband spent his family grocery money to buy a necklace for his mistress. It is no different. Don't rob your wife and children to feed your lusts and don't rob God to feed them, either. Give to God what is due: worship (praise, tithes, thanksgiving) and service. If you spend your time, treasure, and talent on other loves, then you commit idolatry and you betray the Lord. Blessed are the pure in heart, for they shall see God.

Seeing God

The connection between purity of heart and seeing God is well-established in Scripture. The Book of Hebrews says:

> Strive for peace with everyone, and for the *holiness without which no one will see the Lord.* (Hebrews 12:14, ESV, emphasis mine)

Holiness means "set apart" or "distinct." To a people living in a land of idols, we have to come out in order to see God. That is the call of God in the Book of Revelation:

> Then I heard another voice from heaven saying, "Come out of her, my people, lest you take part in

her sins, lest you share in her plagues." (Revelation 18:4, ESV)

In the Book of Revelation, the people of God are beset by a variety of enemies. There is, of course, the devil behind them all, but he works through various lesser agencies to attempt to lure the people of God into destruction. One of these agents is called the Whore of Babylon. This is heavily symbolic language, of course; the actual city of Babylon was at this time little more than an abandoned village on the edge of the desert. By calling her the Whore of Babylon, the Book of Revelation is referring back to the time of the exile, the time looked forward to in Deuteronomy 4, quoted above:

> But from there you will seek the Lord your God and you will find him, if you search after him with all your heart and with all your soul. (Deuteronomy 4:29, ESV)

Babylon had become a symbol for living among seductive idols. Most commentators see behind this symbolic language a warning against seducing culture. The devil uses the allurements of culture to clutter the heart and affection of the believer. He doesn't suggest directly that you abandon God, only that you also worship pleasure, that you make some room in your heart for the pursuit of money and the gratification of the flesh. He says, "Worship God, of course! No one wants you to be a barbarian! But within reason. Go to church on Sunday and hit the bar on Friday. Give something to the church, of course, but spend a little on yourself as well. Buy that new car, indulge that shopper's itch and pay yourself a little as well." This is the seductive voice of Babylon and she whispers into every believer's heart with the siren song of doom. Come out from her. Be holy. Be separate. Be singular and you will see God.

At the end of Revelation, we see the people of God who have resisted every seductive call. They have overcome their enemies by the blood of the lamb and the word of their testimony. Listen to how these folks are symbolically described:

> Then I looked, and behold, on Mount Zion stood the Lamb, and with him 144,000 who had his name and his Father's name written on their foreheads. And I heard a voice from heaven like the roar of many waters and like the sound of loud thunder. The voice I heard was like the sound of harpists playing on their harps, and they were singing a new song before the throne and before the four living creatures and before the elders. No one could learn that song except the 144,000 who had been redeemed from the earth. It is these who have not defiled themselves with women, for *they are virgins*. It is these who follow the Lamb wherever he goes. These have been redeemed from mankind as firstfruits for God and the Lamb, and *in their mouth no lie was found*, for they are blameless. (Revelation 14:1–5, ESV, emphasis mine)

The whole elect people of God, Old Covenant and New, enjoy an intimate fellowship with God around the throne. They sing in perfect harmony a song that no one could know except them because they are those who have loved the Father when all the world called to them to love something else. Look at how they are described: "they are virgins," and "in their mouth no lie was found."

What does this mean? This cannot mean that the only saved people in eternity are virgins. For one thing, that would mean that Peter, James, John, and all the other disciples would be excluded, as the Bible says they were married men. The Apostle Paul laments that of the Apostles only he and Barnabas travel about without a wife. Are we to assume that only Paul and Barnabas are in heaven? David is excluded? Moses? Abraham? No, of course not. If we were to take this verse in a woodenly literal way, poor Abraham would be doubly excluded, for he was both married and a frequent liar!

There is a helpful clue here in the Greek. The phrase "they have not defiled themselves with women" would be the typical way of speaking about sexual sin for men. But then it says, "for they are virgins," using the Greek word *parthenoi*, which literally means "unmarried daughters." So these people are described in both female and male terms. That alone should let us know we are dealing in symbol; it can't be literal because it makes no grammatical sense! In English, if I said, "She is my favourite brother," you would know I was speaking in some form of code, meaning my brother is a bit feminine or my wife is like a brother to me. I can't mean it literally because it makes no literal sense. So here, this is obvious symbol. We must remember that much of the imagery in the Book of Revelation is borrowed from the Old Testament, and virginity in the Old Testament was regularly used of the whole people of God as a symbol for covenant allegiance and singular love and fidelity. As, for example, in 2 Kings 19:21:

> This is the word which the Lord has spoken concerning him: "The virgin, the daughter of Zion, has despised you, laughed you to scorn; the daughter of Jerusalem has shaken her head behind your back!" (2 Kings 19:21, NKJV)

In this passage, "the virgin" meant the whole nation of Judah, which in God's judgment hadn't abandoned the covenant as had her sister, Northern Israel. Thus, virgin meant "covenant allegiance" or "faithfulness." So what we are to see in Revelation 14 is that the elect people of God are those who have not betrayed their allegiance to God by whoring about with the idols and passions of the world. The saved people of God are singular in their allegiance and steadfast in the truth. They have not believed the lies that the devil and his henchmen have been using to ensnare the unsaved who did not love the truth. They didn't "sleep around" with other idols and they held fast to the one truth of the Gospel. These people, the *pure in heart*, see God. That, by the way, is the climactic promise of Revelation. In Revelation 22, after all the enemies of God's people have been thrown down and the elect are gathered into God's eternal presence, look at how this blessed reality is described:

> Then the angel showed me the river of the water of life, bright as crystal, flowing from the throne of God and of the Lamb through the middle of the street of the city; also, on either side of the river, the tree of life with its twelve kinds of fruit, yielding its fruit each month. The leaves of the tree were for the healing of the nations. No longer will there be anything accursed, but the throne of God and of the Lamb will be in it, and his servants will worship him. *They will see his face*, and his name will be on their foreheads. And night will be no more. They will need no light of lamp or sun, for the Lord God will be their light, and they will reign forever and ever. (Revelation 22:1–5, ESV, emphasis mine)

They will see his face! Those who came out of the whore, resisted her seductions, lived holy, and lived with singular devotion and undivided loyalty to God through Jesus Christ, these people *see the face of God!* And his name is on their foreheads. In life, they loved him with all their hearts and all their minds, and in eternity they see him and his name is on their foreheads. They shall be as they have ever been by his electing grace: focused and set apart unto the service and worship of God. Blessed are the pure in heart, for they shall see God.

Small Group Discussion

The sixth beatitude says, *"Blessed are the pure in heart for they shall see God."* As always, the issue of ethics (how we should live and behave) is connected to eschatology (some promise or description of ultimate and end-time reality). Our desire to see God in the end should help us live with singular devotion in the present. Let's read the texts below to continue that conversation, and then, having read the texts, take some time to address the comprehension task that follows.

> Matthew 5:8
> Genesis 3:1–24
> Exodus 33:18–23
> 2 Corinthians 3:12–18
> Hebrews 4:14–16
> 1 John 3:21
> Hebrews 9:11–15
> Job 19:25–27
> Revelation 21:16

Take a moment to consider the twelve statements below. Circle all that you think correctly reflect what the Bible says about being pure in heart.

1. By becoming increasingly singular in our devotion to God, we obtain salvation.
2. We were created for intimacy with God. Sin disrupted that unity and has made us aliens and strangers to God as a race of men.
3. Because of human sinfulness, even the greatest of men and women couldn't see God before the saving work of Jesus on the cross.
4. When we are saved by grace and the perfect blood of Jesus is applied to our hearts, we have a new boldness to enter God's presence in prayer and worship.
5. When we get saved, we are immediately changed and become entirely pure in the eyes of God. We will enjoy perfect communion with God from that point forward all the way to the grave.
6. Even as saved people, sin creates disruption in our communion with God.
7. The work of the Holy Spirit in us as we learn to see Jesus and turn away from evil things is to make us progressively more pure.
8. Knowing that we will see God at the end of life makes us better able to persevere in faith and devotion through difficult times.
9. One of the ways that our saving faith is shown to be real and authentic is that it so fills our heart as to force out every other allegiance.
10. A person who has made a confession of faith but who listens to his wife as though she were his God is not yet a truly converted person.
11. A person who has made a confession of faith and yet who remains perpetually under the power of a fleshy addiction (alcohol, pornography, materialism) can be understood as truly converted

12. A truly converted person keeps God at the centre of his or her heart and is able to find God's voice and follow it, even though he or she lives in a land filled with idols.

Personal Reflection and Evaluation

The Bible says:

> But be doers of the word, and not merely hearers who deceive themselves. For if any are hearers of the word and not doers, they are like those who look at themselves in a mirror; for they look at themselves and, on going away, immediately forget what they were like. But those who look into the perfect law, the law of liberty, and persevere, being not hearers who forget but doers who act— *they will be blessed in their doing.* (James 1:22-25, emphasis mine)

The beatitudes are a description of what *every* Christian should look like. We would be the greatest of fools not to ask a simple follow up question: "To what extent do I look this way? Am I pure in heart?"

Take some time to carefully consider the following ten statements. If the statement is *always true of you,* give yourself a score of ten. If it is *sometimes true of you,* give yourself a five. If it is *rarely or never true of you,* give yourself a zero. Tally your score out of a hundred when you have completed the exercise.

1. When I make a decision as to whether something is right or wrong, I immediately consult the Scriptures so that I may know what God would have me do and think.
2. I will not do something I know God doesn't want me to do because it will please my husband/wife, make me more money, gain me more fame, or satisfy my lusts.
3. My goal in life is to glorify God and enjoy him forever. I have a job, but it is not my goal in life to succeed or make money. I have a family, but my goal in life is not to be the world's greatest husband or father. My goal is to glorify God and enjoy him forever. Everything else I do flows out of that central and determining objective.
4. When I lie in bed, drifting off to sleep, my thoughts do not default to the gratification of my lusts or the accumulation of wealth.
5. I live visibly and boldly as a child of God even when it costs me money, respect, acclaim, or popularity with other people.
6. I am not presently under the domination of any fleshy addiction. I am colouring inside the lines in terms of sexuality and consumption of things.
7. I feel a strong longing in my heart for a deeper communion with God. I feel myself being drawn deeper into his Word, deeper into prayer, deeper into worship, and deeper into loving service.
8. I feel a strong longing for heaven. I am not trying to escape this world, but rather I long for the intimacy that is promised to those who are saved by grace and walk in holiness. I want to behold his face.
9. When I get to heaven, it will not be to see Aunt Margaret or Cousin Tim; I want to see *Jesus!*
10. I often find that my anticipation of heaven influences my decisions here on earth. It affects what I watch on TV, who I listen to, and where I go.

The Narrow Way

My score out of 100: _____

Evaluated on this date: _____

My prayer of honest response to the Lord:

_____

_____

_____

_____

_____

Chapter Seven

Blessed Are the Peacemakers, for They Shall Be Called Sons of God

We mustn't think that being a peacemaker means simply being one of those soft-spoken people who avoids conflict at all costs. Jesus himself doesn't seem to have been one of those people. He didn't avoid conflict at all costs. In fact, several times he appears to instigate conflict and to exacerbate differences. This is the man who went into the temple with a whip, according to John's Gospel:

> In the temple he found those who were selling oxen and sheep and pigeons, and the money-changers sitting there. And making a whip of cords, he drove them all out of the temple, with the sheep and oxen. And he poured out the coins of the money-changers and overturned their tables. And he told those who sold the pigeons, "Take these things

away; do not make my Father's house a house of trade." His disciples remembered that it was written, "Zeal for your house will consume me." (John 2:14–17, ESV)

This is not a man who avoided conflict. He was also not a man to minimize differences when they legitimately existed. Consider this exchange from Luke 11:

> Woe to you Pharisees! For you love the best seat in the synagogues and greetings in the marketplaces. Woe to you! For you are like unmarked graves, and people walk over them without knowing it."
> One of the lawyers answered him, "Teacher, in saying these things you insult us also." (Luke 11:43–45, ESV)

Now, if Jesus were a person who wanted to bring everyone together and minimize differences, he might have backed off here. He might have tried to build an alliance with the scribes against the Pharisees. He might have tried to build a bridge. Instead he said:

> "*Woe to you lawyers also*! For you load people with burdens hard to bear, and you yourselves do not touch the burdens with one of your fingers. Woe to you! For you build the tombs of the prophets whom your fathers killed…Woe to you lawyers! For you have taken away the key of knowledge. You did not enter yourselves, and you hindered those who were entering."
> As he went away from there, the scribes and the Pharisees began to press him hard and to

provoke him to speak about many things, lying in wait for him, to catch him in something he might say. (Luke 11:46–47, 52–54, ESV, emphasis mine)

Jesus clearly didn't wander around avoiding conflict and trying to build bridges where they should not and could not be built. He wasn't always a uniter; often he was a divider. He said so himself:

> Do not think that I have come to bring peace to the earth. I have not come to bring peace, but a sword. For I have come to set a man against his father, and a daughter against her mother, and a daughter-in-law against her mother-in-law. And a person's enemies will be those of his own household. Whoever loves father or mother more than me is not worthy of me, and whoever loves son or daughter more than me is not worthy of me. And whoever does not take his cross and follow me is not worthy of me. (Matthew 10:34–38, ESV)

Whatever we may say about Jesus, it doesn't seem that we may say that he sought peace for peace's sake or that he avoided conflict at all costs. But neither may we say that he was an agitator for agitation's sake or a divider for division's sake. In the Book of Job, there is a lovely phrase, much appreciated by John Calvin.

> "Behold, happy is the man whom God corrects; Therefore do not despise the chastening of the Almighty. *For He bruises, but He binds up; He wounds, but His hands make whole.* (Job 5:17–18, NKJV, emphasis mine)

When God wounds, it is to make whole. When he bruises, it is not the end of his work, but only the beginning. He is like a surgeon who must cut in order to save. Jesus is that kind of peacemaker. He's not interested in Band-Aid solutions; he's performing radical, lifesaving surgery and is often bloody in so doing. Jesus didn't come to offer a course correction or a few words of pithy advice. He came to rescue the perishing and to bind up *the broken*. He was that kind of peacemaker. He made peace through the cross—health through death. The Bible says:

> Therefore remember that at one time you Gentiles in the flesh, called "the uncircumcision" by what is called the circumcision, which is made in the flesh by hands—remember that you were at that time separated from Christ, alienated from the commonwealth of Israel and strangers to the covenants of promise, having no hope and without God in the world. But now in Christ Jesus you who once were far off have been brought near by the blood of Christ. *For he himself is our peace*, who has made us both one and has broken down in his flesh the dividing wall of hostility by abolishing the law of commandments and ordinances, that he might create in himself one new man in place of the two, so making peace, *and might reconcile us both to God in one body through the cross, thereby killing the hostility*. And *he came and preached peace* to you who were far off and peace to those who were near. For through him we both have access in one Spirit to the Father. So then you are no longer strangers and aliens, but you are fellow citizens with the saints and members of the household of God, built on the foundation of the apostles and

prophets, Christ Jesus himself being the cornerstone, in whom the whole structure, being joined together, grows into a holy temple in the Lord. In him you also are being built together into a dwelling place for God by the Spirit. (Ephesians 2:11–22, ESV, emphasis mine)

That's what the Bible means when it talks about peacemaking. Jesus is our peace. The cross is our reconciliation. We forget sometimes as Christians that God was once against us, just as we were against God. The Bible teaches this clearly:

> But God shows his love for us in that *while we were still sinners, Christ died for us.* Since, therefore, we have now been justified by his blood, *much more shall we be saved by him from the wrath of God.* For if *while we were enemies we were reconciled to God* by the death of his Son, much more, now that we are reconciled, shall we be saved by his life. More than that, we also rejoice in God through our Lord Jesus Christ, through whom we have now received reconciliation. (Romans 5:8–11, ESV, emphasis mine)

The Bible is absolutely clear on this: while we were sinners, we were the enemies of God. He was opposed to us. We were under wrath and it was while we were enemies that God effected *reconciliation—he made peace* through the body of Jesus Christ on the cross. We were enemies and strangers, but now we're friends and children. This's why, when Jesus finished his work on the cross and rose from the dead, he greeted the disciples several times by saying, *"Peace be with you"* (Luke 24:36, John 20:19). He wasn't just saying hello; he was saying that because of what he had done for us on the cross, we could have peace—peace with God and peace with one another.

At the very centre of the Christian faith lies the conviction that what Christ accomplished on the cross, if appropriated by faith, secures our peace both with God and with our fellow man. Part of coming to faith is coming to grips with the devastating and alienating nature of sin. Before you turn to Jesus, you turn away from sin because you come to see how it has ruined your life, your relationships, and the relationships of everyone else on the planet. Sin doesn't just impact your relationship with God; it influences your relationship with other people. James, the brother of the Lord said:

> What causes quarrels and what causes fights among you? Is it not this, that your passions are at war within you? You desire and do not have, so you murder. You covet and cannot obtain, so you fight and quarrel. (James 4:1–2, ESV)

According to the Bible, all conflict and quarrelling can be traced back to sinful and selfish desires. The wisdom of the world says that you should do whatever you want as long as it doesn't hurt anyone else. How naive! Eventually all of my selfish wants result in the robbing and harming of other people! We lie to ourselves and hide from the truth that we simply cannot anticipate how our desires impact other people, so we pretend it must be benevolent. We live large, fat, luxurious lifestyles (not hurting anyone else, of course!) and tell each other that we want everyone in the world to do as well as we are and yet we don't stop to consider the math that suggests it would take the resources of four to five planet earths to extend the average middle-class American lifestyle to every family on the planet. It can't be done! Our excess *means their poverty!*

Or consider the sexual lusts. A young man tells himself that pornography is a sin that hurts no one. After all, it's just him and his computer screen. How can it be a crime if there are no victims? Of course, the father whose sixteen-year-old daughter is seduced into the adult film industry by promises of easy money and who becomes a drug addict and an HIV sufferer is never introduced to the young man, so he closes his eyes and pretends he lives in a world without victims.

Wake up! We cannot give vent to sinful passions because they *do* hurt other people, whether we see them or not. Sin is the reason we were enemies of God and sin is the reason we hurt other people. To be a peacemaker is not to avoid that; it is not to hide in the shadows and hope that everyone gets along. To be a peacemaker is *to preach the Gospel!* That's what the Bible says:

> As it is written: "How beautiful are the feet of those who *preach the gospel of peace*, Who bring glad tidings of good things!" (Romans 10:15, NKJV)

Being a peacemaker means that you make the Gospel message of reconciliation your life's work! You take it wherever you go. When you go to work, you go as an undercover Gospel agent. When you coach soccer in the neighbourhood, you coach as an undercover Gospel agent. Your life's work is to see people find peace with God and with one another through the shed blood of Jesus on the cross. Does this mean you preach the Gospel when you're supposed to be making widgets on the line? No. Make widgets. Make widgets as a Gospel man or woman. Demonstrate the peace of God in your conduct. The other widget makers will wonder why you don't hate the boss like they do. They will wonder why you have more money left at the end of pay cycle than they do and they will wonder why you love your wife and get to actually live in the same house as your kids. You tell them about Jesus when they ask. You say, "I don't hate the boss because I know I'm lazy by nature and I work better when there's someone watching over me or I'd probably take a nap in the machinery. That doesn't bother me. I'm pretty honest about my own sin and shortcomings and I appreciate all the helps God gives me to live better. The boss, the cop, the judge… they are ministers of God and it doesn't bother me."

That will start a conversation. When they ask why you have money left over, you can say, "By God's grace, I have fewer lusts everyday that need to be fed. I'm pretty content with what I have, so I'm not buying lottery tickets. I'm pretty happy, so I'm not drowning my sorrows in booze. I like my wife, so I'm not dropping big money at the strip joint. Happiness is cheaper in the long run and God has made me happy and content."

When they tell you about the kids they see once a month and ask why you still live with yours, you can tell them, "My wife and I used to argue a lot, too, but then with God's help I realised that a marriage won't work when you look at each other as servants created to meet your needs. I started looking at my wife as someone to serve, protect, and provide for and left the rest up to God through prayer. It made a huge difference and she started treating me a lot better after that. It had to start with me, though. God fixed me and tempered my expectations and then everything else kind of fell into place. Now we really appreciate each other and we get to live in the same house and I get to be a dad to my kids." Those are Gospel stories that lead back to the cross. You tell those stories and you will be a peacemaker.

Given the sensitivity of this issue in modern-day evangelicalism, we cannot simply define the peacemaking ministry and directly move on to the reward of the peacemaker. There is a great battle being fought inside the church as to whether peacemaking is really a Biblical way of talking at all. The question is often asked this way: "I'm struggling with this idea that Jesus saves us from the wrath of God. How can God save us from God? Why does God have to make peace between us and God? Was God really angry with us before we became Christians? That doesn't sound loving. I read in a Christian book recently that this idea of God saving us from himself is not really Biblical. What gives?"

Let's attempt to address this directly, but humbly. This whole issue of "propitiation"—or God saving us from the wrath of God through Jesus—has again become a debated issue within Christendom. Let's begin by dealing with what the Bible says about it. In Romans 3, we read:

> But now the righteousness of God apart from the law is revealed, being witnessed by the Law and the Prophets, even the righteousness of God, through faith in Jesus Christ, to all and on all who believe. For there is no difference; for all have sinned and fall short of the glory of God, being justified freely by His grace through the redemption that is in Christ Jesus, whom God set forth as a propitiation by His blood, through faith, to demonstrate His righteousness, because in His forbearance God had passed over the sins that were previously committed, to demonstrate at the present time His righteousness, that He might be just and the justifier of the one who has faith in Jesus. (Romans 3:21–26, NKJV)

This is arguably, the holy centre of Christian theology, so we will go slow and break this titanic teaching down concept by concept. First of all, we need to deal with these words:

> But now the righteousness of God apart from the law is revealed… (Romans 3:21a, NKJV)

When we look at the cross, the Bible says that the first thing we should see is the righteousness of God. What does the word righteousness mean? It's the Greek word *dikahyosoonay* and it means "equity," "fairness," or "righteousness." We are supposed to look at the cross and see there the fairness, the altogether rightness, of God. The word also means "justification," a word which implies that we're also looking at the way God establishes our rightness or good standing before him.

As the passage goes on and elaborates, we learn that when we look at the cross, we are to see two things: we are to see and agree that God is fair. He doesn't let go of his holiness in order to show forth love. He is not permissive or weak. He is altogether right and just, even in his demonstrations of love and mercy. And we are also to see the means of our right standing, the means of our legal standing before God.

All of this happens, Paul tells us, "apart from the law." What does he mean by that? Well, he means to inform us that the law isn't a way of salvation. It was never meant to be. The law is not meant by God to save us; the law was given to saved people to reveal God's character and the way in which they should walk. Now, Paul, a good Jewish rabbi, is eager to remind people that this is not new teaching. In fact, he says that this is entirely consistent with the Old Testament:

> …being witnessed by the Law and the Prophets (Romans 3:21b, NKJV.)

The Old Testament taught this whether you saw it there or not. In case you doubt this and think that the Old Testament teaches that the law is a means of salvation, as some poorly informed Christians will say, let me ask you a question: when did the Jews receive the law? Before or after they were a redeemed people? *After.* They were saved in the event of the Exodus. Paul says they were baptised under Moses as they passed through the Red Sea. That was their salvation moment, and only after they were a saved people did God give them the law, so that they could know him and walk in his ways.

Many Christians are confused about this. They think that the New Testament way of salvation is different than the Old Testament way, but Paul says they are the same. Many Christians also think that being saved makes the law irrelevant and they will quote verses like this to try and prove it. But in this very passage Paul corrects that view. In Romans 3:31, he concludes his teaching by saying:

> Do we then overthrow the law by this faith? By no means! On the contrary, we uphold the law.

Paul says, "Our saving faith doesn't overthrow the law! On the contrary, it is only saved people who can uphold the law!" Let me make it really simple: the law is *only* helpful to saved people. After you get saved, the Holy Spirit helps you walk in God's ways. Before you are saved, the law only condemns and frustrates you. It's a help to the saved and a deadly burden to the unsaved.

Paul goes on to say:

> …even the righteousness of God, through faith in Jesus Christ, to all and on all who believe… (Romans 3:22, NKJV)

So, this justification of people by God is applied to those who believe—or, rather, as it says in the original Greek, upon those "who are believing." Those who are believing—we might say, "those who are walking in faith"—are under the saving application of the blood of Jesus. It doesn't say that it is applied to those who once felt kindly inclined towards Jesus at a campfire; it says it is applied to those who are walking in faith.

Here we encounter the difficulty of capturing in English what the Bible means by "faith" and "belief." In English, our word "believe" tends to mean an intellectual decision. In my mind, it is firmly established that Jesus died on the cross. But we all know that the Bible is at great pains to help us understand that *faith*, or saving *belief*, means more than that. The devil in hell believes that Jesus died on the cross. He has determined that issue in his mind. Is he under the saving application of the cross? No. So what does it mean to believe? Let's ask the Bible. John 3:36 says:

> Whoever believes in the Son has eternal life; whoever disobeys the Son will not see life, but must endure God's wrath. (John 3:36)

According to the Gospel of John, what is the opposite of believing? Is it "not believing"? No, according to this verse, the opposite of believing is *disobeying*. That is why Jesus said:

> You are my friends if you do what I command you. (John 15:14)

To have faith in Jesus, to have a relationship with Jesus, is therefore a commitment to *walk in his ways*. If you define faith or belief in any other way, you're in disagreement with Jesus and in company with demons. It is to those walking in faith, following Jesus, who are under the application of this grace.

Paul goes on to say in Romans 3:

> For there is no difference; for all have sinned and fall short of the glory of God… (Romans 3:22–23, NKJV)

The need for this salvation is universal. Whether you are a good Jew or a bad Jew, whether you are a good Gentile or a bad Gentile, whether you are a nice person or an evil person, *you need this gift of God to be justified in his presence.*

This right here is the battleground when witnessing to modern day people. Does Ghandi need this gift in order to enter heaven and live in God's presence? Yes! Does a really nice person who gives money to the United Way and lives a moral life need this gift of God to enter heaven? Yes! There is no one who doesn't need it because *all* are sinners and *all* fall short of the glory of God.

We are so inclined to take pride in our works of righteousness and so incredibly blind to our acts of death and destruction. Human beings are notorious for overestimating their own goodness and for underestimating the impact of their own selfishness and pride. How many self-satisfied, falsely confident North Americans are out there driving around in their giant SUVs, living in their tidy McMansions, eating their quarter pounders, and watching their TVs who have *no concept* of the damage their lifestyle is doing to innocent people on the other side of the planet? They think themselves righteous. They think themselves innocent. They're filled with *pride* and *blind* to their own culpability, and this verse sticks a finger in their chests and says, "You need this, make no mistake." There is no salvation without humility and confession. You need this. I need this. Ghandi needed this. All have sinned.

> ...being justified freely by His grace... (Romans 3:24, NKJV)

All salvation begins with the grace of God. None of us had a hope before grace. We were dead in the water, with no means of progress in salvation, until God so loved the world that he *gave*. There's no room for pride or boasting in the kingdom of God. We are all here by grace.

> ...through the redemption that is in Christ Jesus. (Romans 3:24, NKJV)

What does this mean? Redemption means simply to purchase one's freedom. It implies that a price has been paid. Salvation is free for us, but it cost God dearly. God paid the price of his Son Jesus Christ to set us free. Look at the cross and see your value. You mean enough to God that he would die to know you. More than that, he would kill to love you. For, make no mistake, it was the love of God *for you* that nailed Jesus to that cross. It was not the Romans who killed Jesus, and it was not the Jews. God killed him because he loved you. He would die for you, and he would kill for you. In our culture, we pay shrinks and cranks millions of dollars to help us rediscover our self-esteem and self-worth. Save your money and consider the body of Jesus Christ upon the cross.

But before we leave this verse, we must also ask in what ways we are free. The Apostle Paul and the author of Hebrews suggest the metaphor of the Exodus for understanding our freedom. How many times were the Hebrews set free? Well, in a primary sense they were set free once. God walked them out of Egypt, through the Red Sea, and destroyed the enemy that had held them captive. In the same way, we have been set free from the kingdom and lordship of Satan and been made citizens of the kingdom of God. We are free. Hebrews 2 states it this way:

> Since, therefore, the children share flesh and blood, he himself likewise shared the same things, so that through death he might destroy the one who has the power of death, that is, the devil, and free those who all their lives were held in slavery by the fear of death. (Hebrews 2:14–15)

The cross sets us free from the dominion of the devil and releases us from hell and the fear of hell. The perfect love of God, displayed on the cross, frees us from fear and allows us to live sacrificially. Having no fear of death and hell, we can use our remaining time on earth to serve the Lord and others knowing that we will live forever with him in eternity. That is the primary way of understanding our freedom, but there's more. D.A. Carson, professor of the New Testament at Trinity Evangelical Divinity College, refers to redemption as "freedom in layers." Let's go back to our Exodus analogy. How many times were the Jews set free? Once—sort of. The power of Pharaoh over them was broken once and for all in decisive fashion… *but* the hold of Egypt over them—*inside them*—took years to overcome.

> The Israelites said to them, "If only we had died by the hand of the Lord in the land of Egypt, *when we sat by the fleshpots and ate our fill of bread*; for you have brought us out into this wilderness to kill this whole assembly with hunger." (Exodus 16:3, emphasis mine)

The first time dinner doesn't arrive on time, the Israelites start fantasizing about Egypt.

"Remember Egypt, Phil?"

"Do I?! It was awesome! We use to sit around the buffet table and stuff our faces until we passed out on our giant pillows. Those were good times. I wish we were there now."

Really? Egypt was a giant buffet table? I don't think so. The memory of sin is always distorted. When you're new in faith, the call of sin is still strong. You're free from the devil, but he still speaks out of your flesh and into your soul. He whispers to you, "Remember heroin? Oh, those were good times. It was like riding a cloud through a carnival of cotton candy wearing loose-fitting pants and comfy shoes," Yeah, it wasn't quite like that. He doesn't remind you of that time you almost choked to death on your own vomit, or the fact that Children's Aid took your kids away or that you had to sell your body into slavery to ensure your supply—all of that is left out and Egypt becomes heaven and heaven becomes hell. It takes a while to be set free from Egypt in your soul. You're free, though it may take a while to feel and live free. But the same Jesus who set you free is, indeed, working in you to set you free in experience. Redemption in layers.

In Romans 3:25, Paul takes us into the deep waters. Speaking of Jesus and his death on the cross, he says:

> …whom God set forth as a propitiation by His blood, through faith… (NKJV)

Propitiation is a word we don't use much in English. It is the Greek word *hilastayreeon*, and it's a word which references the mercy seat where sacrifices were made in the Old Testament. It's a sacrifice which turns away the wrath of God and invites his favour.

Now, a lot of people don't like this word. A lot of modern Bible translations intentionally avoid this word because they shy away from the implication that before we are covered by the blood of Jesus we are under the wrath of God. In the video promo for the controversial and tragically heretical book *Love Wins*, by Rob Bell, the author asks some pretty alarming questions:

> And then there is the question behind the questions, the real question: What is God like? Because millions of millions of people were taught that the primary message—the center of the Gospel of Jesus—is that God is going to send you to hell, unless you believe in Jesus. And so, what gets, subtly, sort of caught and taught is that Jesus rescues you from God. *But what kind of God is that, that we would need to be rescued from this God?* How could that God ever be good? How could that God ever be trusted? And how could that ever be good news? (emphasis mine)

What kind of God is that? The Bible kind. Jesus said:

> Whoever believes in the Son has eternal life; whoever does not obey the Son shall not see life, but the wrath of God *remains on him*. (John 3:36, ESV, emphasis mine)

The Apostle Paul teaches this same thing in Ephesians:

> All of us once lived among them in the passions of our flesh, following the desires of flesh and senses,

> and *we were by nature children of wrath, like everyone else.* (Ephesians 2:3, emphasis mine)

> Let no one deceive you with empty words, for because of these things *the wrath of God comes on those who are disobedient.* Therefore do not be associated with them. (Ephesians 5:6–7, emphasis mine)

Make no mistake, the Bible says that if you aren't under the blood of Christ, you're under the wrath of God. The word "propitious" means "favourable" in English. A sacrifice of propitiation then means a sacrifice that changes how we experience God. Before it, we know his wrath; after it, we know only favour. We aren't left to wonder whether this is what Paul means in Romans 3, because he tells us plainly just two chapters later:

> But God proves his love for us in that while we still were sinners Christ died for us. Much more surely then, now that we have been justified by his blood, *will we be saved through him from the wrath of God.* (Romans 5:8–9, emphasis mine)

What are we saved from, friends? The false shepherds and false prophets would have you believe that you're saved from yourself, that you're saved from your bad habits. Some will go so far as to say you're saved from the church and the "religious people," but what does the Bible say? What are we saved from? The wrath of God. We need peace with God. Only after we have that do we find peace with ourselves and with one another.

When you consider the body of Christ on the cross, understand that for you, it changes everything. You know God now not as an angry judge but as a loving father. The cross has turned wrath into favour, praise to his name!

Why must this be so? Have you wondered that? Why is the cross necessary? It's one thing to know what it accomplishes, and quite another to know why it's necessary. Now Paul tells us, saying that it was:

> …to demonstrate His righteousness, because in His forbearance God had passed over the sins that were previously committed, to demonstrate at the present time His righteousness, that He might be just and the justifier of the one who has faith in Jesus. (Romans 3:25–26, NKJV)

The cross was necessary because God decided that it was. Understand this, friend: God orchestrated every event in the life, death, and resurrection of Jesus to fulfill what he deemed necessary to maintain his holiness while securing our salvation. The Old Testament, too, affirms this:

> Yet *it was the will of the Lord to crush him* with pain. When *you make his life an offering for sin.* (Isaiah 53:10, emphasis mine)

You see, God had a problem. He created this world as a reflection of his glory and nature. It was knit together with the very fabric of his holiness. It is replete with moral laws and analogies. Within this world, he planted humankind, desiring to have a relationship with them that also reflected his character of love and holiness. He gave them moral consciousness so that they could see and appreciate his holiness and he gave them moral will so that they could love him truly. But human beings exercised their moral freedom and rejected God's holiness, believing the lie that they could be like God, deciding right and wrong for themselves.

So, God had a choice. He could have destroyed this world and every human being with it and started over, or he could come up with a means of restoring all things to their proper design and intention. The cross is God's plan. This is God's re-creative, universally corrective solution. The plan, hidden in the mind of God from eternity past, is now manifest, thrust forth, displayed in glory upon the cross. It was to show himself *righteous* because, observing the outworking of this plan, an angel might have asked, "How is it, Holy God, that sinful men such as Moses and Elijah and Abraham are permitted into heaven? They carry their sin and they are in all ways sons of Adam." A fair question and one obviously considered. The Apostle Paul says in Ephesians 3:

> This grace was given to me to bring to the Gentiles the news of the boundless riches of Christ, and *to make everyone see* what is the plan of the mystery hidden for ages in God who created all things; so that through the church the wisdom of God in its rich variety might now *be made known to the rulers and authorities in the heavenly places.* This was in accordance with the eternal purpose that he has carried out in Christ Jesus our Lord, in whom we have access to God in boldness and confidence through faith in him. (Ephesians 3:8-12, emphasis mine)

"Just you watch," says God. "I have a plan that will preserve my holiness and standards of justice while at the same time purchasing back a people for myself." *God always gets what he wants.* Jesus came and lived a perfect life, and because he was perfect his *life* satisfied the holiness of God. His blood was therefore infinitely valuable to God. We know this from Leviticus 17:14:

> For *the life of every creature—its blood is its life*; therefore I have said to the people of Israel: You shall not eat the blood of any creature, for the life of every creature is its blood; whoever eats it shall be cut off. (emphasis mine)

Because Jesus' life was perfect, his blood was infinitely meritorious. If we are under it, if we trust solely in it, then we are paid for, redeemed, and declared innocent before Almighty God. God in the past had overlooked sin. Moses, Abraham, and Elijah were all in heaven before Christ came to earth. God is concerned lest any should ask, "Has the love of God for humankind made obsolete his justice? By what standard of fairness can such men be admitted?" God answers with Jesus. His blood paid for their sins. All those in the Old Testament who looked through the promises of God and who looked through the sacrifices of tent and temple as a window to his ultimate gift of grace were accounted righteous by the blood of the cross. The wages of sin is death; his death paid the wage of their sin, and not only their sin but the sins of all men and women who would by faith are washed in his blood. Our right standing with God is:

> ...by His blood, through faith. (Romans 3:25, NKJV)

By his blood, through faith. If you stand under the blood of the cross, in faith, prepared to take up your cross and follow him, you are paid for. You are free and righteous in the eyes of God. An exchange happens at the cross. A fine is paid and a new status is conferred.

> For our sake he made him to be sin who knew no sin, so that in him we might become the righteousness of God. (2 Corinthians 5:21)

If you have claimed the blood of Christ as your covering and are walking in faith, you have a righteousness before God that is no reflection of your present level of sanctification. Here's what I mean: you are being set free by degrees. We already said that, and you knew it to be true in your life long before I said it. You are *free,* indeed, but becoming free by degree.

Now, take comfort in this: God doesn't view you as in being some process of righteous; he views you as *entirely righteous,* because he has accounted to your ledger the righteousness of Christ. Legally speaking, before God your ledger used to read: "Adulterer, liar, murderer, cheat, fornicator, idolater." The penalty for those sins is death. But God has a very wonderful magic marker filled with the blood of Christ and if you plead for him to do so, he will use that marker on your ledger and, though your sins were as scarlet, he will wash them white as snow. Everything in that ledger disappears and in the place of the word guilty, a new word resides: *Righteous. Welcome. Justified in being here.* You have a right to the presence of God—not a right you earned, but a right you received as grace.

This is the heart of the Gospel and it is glorious Good News. Despite what you may have heard or read recently, peacemaking is still the most important job in the universe. Blessed are the peacemakers, for they shall be called sons of God.

Sons of God

As with most eschatological promises there is a sense in which the thing promised will be realized in an ultimate sense after the Second Coming and the Renewal of all things. Simultaneously, there's a sense in which we have the first fruits, the down payment, the initial experience of the thing promised in the here and now. This beatitude promises:

> Blessed are the peacemakers, for they shall be called sons of God. (Matthew 5:9, ESV)

While I am definitely not a translation Nazi, this is one of those occasions where a literal translation is very helpful. The TNIV translates this as "children of God" and while I sympathize with the awkwardness of gender pronouns in the Bible (so often verses are written as he-this and him-that simply because a gender-neutral way of saying these things doesn't exist), I think this is a place where the maleness of the word has symbolic significance. In that culture, being a son meant two things that are wrapped up in this promise. First of all, it almost certainly implied common vocation with the father. Today it is quite rare to find a person who does for a living what their mother or father did. In those days, it was extremely rare to find someone who did not. A baker's son became a baker and a farmer's son became a farmer. Jesus, in the Bible, is referred to both as "the carpenter's son" (Matthew 13:55) and as "a carpenter" (Mark 6:3), meaning that Jesus, too, adopted the vocation of his father. Therefore to be a "son of God" means that you will be recognized as a person engaged in the same sort of work as God Almighty. When you make the Gospel your life's work, people will see that you are engaged in the same sort of peacemaking that your Father is engaged in. That is almost certainly part of what is implied by the use of the word "son."

The other likely inference relates to inheritance. You will share in the riches and possession of your father in heaven. You will possess things that seem rightly to belong to God. All those who go forth in the work of the Gospel go forth in power that seems rightly to belong only to God. Is not this also part of the Great Commission? Jesus said:

> And Jesus came and spoke to them, saying, "All authority has been given to Me in heaven and on earth. Go therefore and make disciples of all the nations, baptizing them in the name of the Father and of the Son and of the Holy Spirit, teaching them to observe all things that I have commanded you; and lo, I am with you always, even to the end of the age." (Matthew 28:18–20, NKJV)

Jesus has all authority (the Greek word for authority can equally be translated as power) and he sends us out into Gospel work with the promise that, as we are going, he is with us. He is with us *in power* and *authority* as we go. That promise is more explicit in the recollection of the Great Commission in Mark's Gospel:

> "Go into all the world and proclaim the gospel to the whole creation. Whoever believes and is baptized will be saved, but whoever does not believe will be condemned. And these signs will accompany those who believe: in my name they will cast out demons; they will speak in new tongues; hey will pick up serpents with their hands; and if they drink any deadly poison, it will not hurt them;

they will lay their hands on the sick, and they will recover."

So then the Lord Jesus, after he had spoken to them, was taken up into heaven and sat down at the right hand of God. And they went out and preached everywhere, while the Lord worked with them and *confirmed the message by accompanying signs.* (Mark 16:15–20, ESV, emphasis mine)

This isn't the place to discuss how literal or how symbolic this language is meant to be understood (does picking up snakes mean facing spiritual adversaries with confidence?). Rather, the point is that as we go out into Gospel work we take with us signs of God's power and presence. These signs are evidences of our special relationship to God. They mark us as sons. We possess things that are properly understood to belong to God.

Whenever we begin talking about spiritual gifts, certain questions are likely to arise. One common question is: "How prevalent are these signs supposed to be in the present age?" D.A. Carson has a great quote in his book, *How Long, O Lord*. Carson says:

> In this day when many in the Western world have been seduced by some form of the power, health and wealth gospel, it is important to stress the believer's location—between the fall and the new heaven and the new earth, enjoying the "down payment" of the Spirit but by no means free of death and decay.[5]

---

5 Carson, D.A. *How Long, O Lord?* (Grand Rapids, MI: Baker Academic, 2006), p. 223.

It isn't so much "nothing now and everything later" or "everything now and everything later" as much as it is "first fruits now and fullness later." Let me put it this way: we *will* be entirely healed, renewed, and restored in our bodies in the new heaven and the new earth… and we have signs and first fruits of that in the present age. There is a reason that healings are called miracles in the Bible and not Thursday, *because they are not the norm. They are signs, first fruits, and encouragements!* God gives them to us *sometimes* to remind us of all the good that is ahead, to affirm that we are his people doing his business, and to encourage us for the tough times we must yet endure. We are not to expect them always, neither are we to be discouraged if we do not get one when we ask. We mustn't obsess over the signs and first fruits. Let's be future-focused and present-prevailing!

Occasionally, I'll have someone get quite panicky if we haven't had a healing in a few months. They'll begin asking questions like, "Does this imply that there's sin in the camp? Should we bring in a healer to get things going again? Are we lacking in faith?" No. Relax. Take some counsel from the Apostle Peter:

> Beloved, do not think it strange concerning the fiery trial which is to try you, as though some strange thing happened to you; but rejoice to the extent that you partake of Christ's sufferings, that when His glory is revealed, you may also be glad with exceeding joy. (1 Peter 4:12–13, NKJV)

Peter says, "Don't be freaked out by having to actually walk all the way through some trials or hard times. This is not cause for concern. Rather, embrace these trials as an opportunity to know Christ better and to sharpen your anticipation for the full harvest of blessings yet to come." Great counsel!

We pray for healings, first fruits, and signs in our church and we *believe* God gives them. When he gives them, *we rejoice.* It encourages our people and validates our message; it shows that we are sons of our Father doing the Father's business. When he doesn't give them, we don't panic as though something strange were going on. We embrace the trial and all the more eagerly long for his appearing and the renewal of all things. We believe that we have these things now, but we also believe the best is yet to come. As with all the other eschatological promises contained in the various beatitudes, we hold these things in the here and now in a very partial way. Do some move in powerful prophetic gifts that greatly aid in Gospel work and mission? Yes, but as Paul said:

> For we know in part and we prophesy in part, but when the perfect comes, the partial will pass away. (1 Corinthians 13:10, ESV)

In the here and now, we possess these things in a very partial way. When the Lord returns at his Second Coming and restores all things, we will hold all things pertaining to the Father in a complete sense. This, too, is a promise of Scripture:

> For all who are led by the Spirit of God are *sons of God.* For you did not receive the spirit of slavery to fall back into fear, but you have received the Spirit of *adoption as sons*, by whom we cry, "Abba! Father!" The Spirit himself bears witness with our spirit that *we are children of God*, and if children, then heirs—*heirs of God and fellow heirs with Christ*, provided we suffer with him in order that we may also be glorified with him. For I consider that the sufferings of this present time are *not*

> *worth comparing with the glory that is to be revealed to us.* (Romans 8:14–18, ESV, emphasis mine)

The Apostle Paul's argument is that we have been adopted as sons into God's family through Jesus Christ, and that if we are sons than we will certainly inherit! We will share in God's riches to the same extent that Jesus does! What a promise! This promise is so glorious that the Apostle considers the afflictions of this present age very slight indeed when compared to the glory ahead. The greater part of our inheritance is ahead. We do possess great things of God in this present age, but nothing compared to what yet lies ahead. We are sons now, but more lies in the future.

That we shall be sons of God is obviously a promise that as we do Gospel work, as we go about in the family business of peacemaking, we shall be seen as belonging to God and as possessing some of the things of God even in our present estate. It also means that great glories lie ahead for those who persevere in Gospel ministry. There are great riches in heaven for those who persevere in Gospel witness and there is also a more glorious sharing in God's work.

> If we endure, we shall also reign with *him*. (2 Timothy 2:12, ESV, emphasis mine)

The Bible is very clear that those who endure and persevere in Gospel witness will reign with Christ in his kingdom. Consider the glorious promise of Revelation 20:

> Then I saw thrones, and seated on them were those to whom the authority to judge was committed. Also I saw the souls of those who had been beheaded for the testimony of Jesus and for the word of God, and who had not worshiped the

> beast or its image and had not received its mark on their foreheads or their hands. They came to life and reigned with Christ for a thousand years. The rest of the dead did not come to life until the thousand years were ended. This is the first resurrection. Blessed and holy is the one who shares in the first resurrection! Over such the second death has no power, but they will be priests of God and of Christ, and they will reign with him for a thousand years. (Revelation 20:4–6, ESV)

When Christ begins to restore all creation through his benevolent and glorious reign, those who had been beheaded for the testimony of Jesus and for the Word of God (symbolic language for those who have persisted in Gospel ministry despite the cost) shall be resurrected to *reign!* They shall reign with Christ in a fuller, more complete way. They shall share in the work of reconciliation that is and always has been the family business. Thus, when we are promised that as peacemakers we shall be called sons of God, we are promised something wonderful now and unspeakably glorious in the age to come. Let that truth motivate us to persist and persevere in Gospel ministry. Blessed are the peacemakers, for they shall be called sons of God.

Small Group Discussion

The seventh beatitude says, *"Blessed are the peacemakers for they shall be called sons of God."* As always, the issue of ethics (how we should live and behave) is connected to eschatology (some promise or description of ultimate end-time reality). This glorious promise, and indeed this present provision, should equip and inspire us in our Gospel ministry. Let's read the texts below to continue that conversation and then, having read the texts, take some time to address the comprehension task that follows.

> Matthew 5:9
> Genesis 3:1–24
> Romans 3:9–26
> Romans 10:14–15
> Ephesians 2:1–22
> Revelation 20:1–15

Take a moment and consider the fourteen statements below. Circle all that you think correctly reflect what the Bible says about being a peacemaker and a son of God.

1. A peacemaker is likely a nonconfrontational person who shrinks from hostility and wants everyone to get along.
2. We are born in a state of peace with God, but if/when we sin, we become God's enemies.
3. When we begin obeying God's commandments and living holy lives, we become friends and even sons of God.
4. When the infinitely meritorious blood of Jesus is applied to our account by faith, we are declared just in God's eyes and he turns toward us in that moment in friendship and fatherly love.
5. When God converts a human heart by his grace and fills that heart with his Holy Spirit, we are given the potential for peace in our human relationships as sinful lusts and desires begin to fade and come under submission.
6. Being a peacemaker will often involve confrontation with the idols of our world. Unless we shake people free from their idols, they cannot find peace with God and others. Thus, peacemaking often looks violent and contentious at the start of the process.

7. A peacemaker is likely to enjoy the goodwill and favour of humankind. People will generally appreciate someone who is trying to reconcile them to God and to others.
8. Many peacemakers get killed in the crossfire. Peace is often made through death.
9. When you're at peace with God, you find yourself immediately at peace in all your other relationships.
10. Spiritual signs are given so that Christians will not have to suffer the many ills and difficulties that pagans deal with.
11. Power goes with those who preach the Gospel. It might be fair to say that the more your life is given to Gospel ministry, the more you might expect to possess first fruits and signs of the power of God.
12. Spiritual gifts are given to build up the church and have nothing to do with evangelism and Gospel witness.
13. In heaven, everyone is equal and there are no authority structures. Therefore, to reign with Christ means simply to observe or celebrate his reign. We don't exercise authority over anyone, because all are equal.
14. Peacemakers will participate with Christ in the renewing of all things. If you are faithful with a small part of the family business, you will be given much in the age to come.

Personal Reflection and Evaluation

The Bible says:

> But be doers of the word, and not merely hearers who deceive themselves. For if any are hearers of the word and not doers, they are like those who

look at themselves in a mirror; for they look at themselves and, on going away, immediately forget what they were like. But those who look into the perfect law, the law of liberty, and persevere, being not hearers who forget but doers who act— *they will be blessed in their doing.* (James 1:22–25, emphasis mine)

The beatitudes are a description of what *every* Christian should look like. We would be the greatest of fools not to ask a simple follow up question: "To what extent do I look this way? Am I a peacemaker?"

Take some time and carefully consider the following ten statements. If the statement is *always true of you,* give yourself a score of ten. If it is *sometimes true of you,* give yourself a five. If it is *rarely or never true of you,* give yourself a zero. Tally your score out of a hundred when you have completed the exercise.

1. I know what the Gospel is and am eager to share it with others.
2. I'm always praying for opportunities to share the Good News with people.
3. I'm not afraid to confront the idols that are holding a person in bondage. I will wound in order to make whole, if God so directs.
4. My lifestyle invites all manner of questions about the peace I enjoy with God and my fellow man.
5. I am always ready to give an answer for the faith, hope, and peace I have.
6. I experience God's provision of power as I share the Gospel and participate in the Good News ministry.
7. People easily identify me as a Christian by the manner of my life and speech.

8. As I myself come increasingly under the power of the Gospel in my own life, I find myself more and more at peace with my brothers and sisters in Christ. I am rarely involved in conflict because my desires are in submission to Christ.
9. I find myself more willing to be wronged if it means progress for the Gospel. When wronged at work, I think less about getting justice and more about turning this into a Gospel opportunity.
10. I occasionally face some tribulation and crossfire as a result of my peacemaking activities.

My score out of 100: _____

Evaluated on this date: _____

My prayer of honest response to the Lord:

_____

_____

_____

_____

_____

Chapter Eight

Blessed Are Those Who Are Persecuted for Righteousness' Sake, for Theirs Is the Kingdom of Heaven

The eighth beatitude joins with the first in forming what scholars call an *inclusio*. A careful reading of the beatitudes will reveal that the first and the last are bound to the same promise: *"for theirs is the kingdom of heaven."* The two together serve as bookends marking out the boundaries of the fully converted life.

As it is true to say that the fully converted life begins with poverty of spirit, so also it is true to say that the fully converted life always ends in persecution. If a person exhibits no poverty of spirit—if he is self-righteous, independent, unrepentant, and cocksure—we would be entirely right to question their salvation. Likewise, if a person has never experienced persecution as a Christian, we would be entirely right to question whether they have ever been properly converted. The Bible teaches this clearly and unambiguously, Jesus said:

> If the world hates you, know that it has hated me before it hated you. If you were of the world, the world would love you as its own; but because you are not of the world, but I chose you out of the world, therefore the world hates you. Remember the word that I said to you: "A servant is not greater than his master." If they persecuted me, they will also persecute you. If they kept my word, they will also keep yours. But all these things they will do to you on account of my name, because they do not know him who sent me. If I had not come and spoken to them, they would not have been guilty of sin, but now they have no excuse for their sin. Whoever hates me hates my Father also. If I had not done among them the works that no one else did, they would not be guilty of sin, but now they have seen and hated both me and my Father. But the word that is written in their Law must be fulfilled: "They hated me without a cause." But when the Helper comes, whom I will send to you from the Father, the Spirit of truth, who proceeds from the Father, he will bear witness about me. And you also will bear witness, because you have been with me from the beginning. (John 15:18–27, ESV)

Jesus says, in essence, "If they hated the first instalment of the message and hated the ultimate messenger, how much more will they hate you as you bring witness to the message and the messenger? Insomuch as you carry on the Gospel ministry, you will share in the same hatred of the world that carried me to the cross."

Indeed, it is impossible to imagine that a person could live a fully converted life, that he would take God at his Word and build his life on God's truth as if it were *the truth*, that he would mourn over the practices and devotions everyone else accepts as normal, that he would long for the things of eternity and be disinterested in the things of this world, that he would forgive and forgo vindication and vengeance (and thereby condemn everyone else for seeking "closure"), that he would be so singular, so uncompromising in his allegiance and that he would see the Gospel as the solution to all of life's conflicts and difficulties, and that he would give himself to preaching the Good News and *not* be hated, reviled, and persecuted for righteousness' sake. That is simply inconceivable. It cannot be done in a world that remains hostile to God. Paul said to Timothy:

> Indeed, all who desire to live a godly life in Christ Jesus will be persecuted. (2 Timothy 3:12, ESV)

The testimony of the Scriptures is clear: the final proof that a person is fully converted is that they attract the animosity of the world. If they do not, the opposite is true; they must be considered as still under the wrath of God. Jesus says that very thing in Luke's recording of the Sermon on the Mount:

> Woe to you, when all people speak well of you, for so their fathers did to the false prophets. (Luke 6:26, ESV)

The word "woe" means "how unfortunate for you!" Why is it unfortunate when all speak well of you? Because it proves you are not saved. It proves you remain under the wrath of God, which is a terrible place to be. Friendship with the world only proves we are the enemies of God:

> You adulterous people! Do you not know that friendship with the world is enmity with God? Therefore whoever wishes to be a friend of the world makes himself an enemy of God. (James 4:4, ESV)

Of course, there are other reasons a person might attract the hostility of the world around them. Not all reviled people are reviled for Jesus' sake. Many "Christians" are reviled because they are mean, disagreeable, contentious, political bullies, finger pointers, hypocrites, and tightwads. If the waitress at the restaurant has bad things to say about Christians, it should be because they don't max out the bar tab… not because they fail to tip. If the boss has bad things to say about Christians, it should be because they won't falsify shipping logs… not because they gossip and show up late for work. If the talk shows have bad things to say about Christians, it should be because we hold crazy ideas like "the sanctity of life"… not because our pastors sleep around or molest children. There are good reasons and bad reasons to attract reviling and persecution. Peter warned his churches about this important distinction:

> If you are insulted for the name of Christ, you are blessed, because the Spirit of glory and of God rests upon you. But let none of you suffer as a murderer or a thief or an evildoer or as a meddler. Yet if anyone suffers as a Christian, let him not be ashamed, but let him glorify God in that name. (1 Peter 4:14–16, ESV)

It is suffering for *Christ* and for *righteousness* that results in our being blessed. This eighth beatitude is the hinge where Jesus transitions out of his discussion of the fully converted life and into a discussion about how that life lived by the people of God functions in a fallen world. It is obviously the climax of the beatitudes and it receives additional content, partly because of its importance and partly because it bridges into the next topic. Jesus goes on to say:

> Blessed are you when others revile you and persecute you and utter all kinds of evil against you falsely on my account. Rejoice and be glad, for your reward is great in heaven, for so they persecuted the prophets who were before you. (Matthew 5:11–12, ESV)

In verse 11, Jesus makes the previous "for righteousness' sake" the equivalent of "on my account," which serves to so thoroughly identify the disciple of Jesus with the practice of his righteousness that there is no place whatsoever for confessed allegiance to Jesus that's not full of following righteousness. To belong to Jesus is to practice righteousness. To love Jesus is to live as he lived and to obey his commandments. There is no such thing as a saved person who walks as he will. Saved people, fully converted people, follow Jesus and as a result they end up as he ended up: carrying a cross. Did not Jesus say that very thing?

> If anyone would come after me, let him deny himself and take up his cross daily and follow me. (Luke 9:23, ESV)

According to this verse, following Jesus is the equivalent of cross-carrying. To follow Jesus is to end up carrying a cross, with all that implies. Stated negatively, Jesus says:

> Whoever does not bear his own cross and come after me cannot be my disciple. (Luke 14:27, ESV)

According to this verse, if a person goes through life and never bears the scorn of the world, never feels the sting of its slander, quite simply he cannot be a disciple of Jesus. It is inconceivable.

Coming to grips with this truth helps us understand why the disciples seemed to take such joy in the experience of persecution. Jesus tells us to rejoice and be exceedingly glad when this happens, but we expect a sort of inner, invisible joy because persecution is generally quite painful. Instead we see the disciples literally feeling *joy* when they get the snot kicked out of them for Jesus. The disciples were once commanded by the Sanhedrin not to preach the Gospel and they were given the synagogue scourging by way of warning. This was no pat on the pants; they were beat on the back of the legs with slender rods. This could leave a man unable to walk and many historians believe that it was what caused Paul to walk with a severe limp. But look at how Luke tells the story:

> when they had called in the apostles, they beat them and charged them not to speak in the name of Jesus, and let them go. Then they left the presence of the council, *rejoicing that they were counted worthy to suffer dishonor for the name.* And every day, in the temple and from house to house, they did not cease teaching and preaching Jesus as the Christ. (Acts 5:40–42, ESV, emphasis mine)

It sounds like they'd be leaping for joy if they could. How is that possible? Why did they treasure this beating? Because it proved the genuineness of their faith and served to strengthen their walk and spiritual empowerment.

This leads us into an area we mustn't avoid given the current trends within contemporary Christendom. After reading what we have said so far in this chapter and after studying the reaction of the disciples, a young believer might ask a question like this one—a question, by the way, I have been asked an awful lot recently: "I am struggling with this issue of assurance of salvation. I was always taught that if you make a sincere profession of faith, you had assurance of salvation. It sounds like you're saying that assurance comes later in the process and is connected to persevering under trial. How does that square with what some call eternal security?"

That's a very timely question, and if you don't agree you probably haven't been talking to very many young Christians or many older Christians whose children made a profession of faith fifteen years ago but have long since walked away. This question matters. Let's try and answer it directly and with humility by first studying what the Word of God has to say. In Luke 21:19, Jesus says:

> By your endurance you will gain your souls.

This verse seems clearly to be teaching something we often refer to as "the perseverance of the saints." The Greek literally says: "In or by your perseverance/patient endurance, you will obtain your souls." Wow. Not "when you raise your hand at the campfire." Not "when you decide in your heart that Jesus died for your sins." But "in persevering under trial, tribulation, and testing, you obtain your soul." That's pretty huge.

This probably isn't the place for a full-length defence of the classic doctrine of the perseverance of the saints, so I'll just give you the short version. The short version is that the Protestant Evangelical Church has historically taught that the primary fruit of faith is perseverance. Meaning, that if a person makes a "decision" for Jesus and tracks for a short while—a year, two years, or more—but then ultimately falls away under persecution or difficulty, and thus fails to show persevering faith, that person *was never saved,* because saving faith, by definition, perseveres under trial and over time. That is the historic evangelical view and I support it one hundred percent. I don't support the more recent, and I believe entirely inadequate, view known as "eternal security," which suggests that everyone who raises their hand or makes a sincere profession of faith is saved for all time despite that they may fall away. I don't care how many people say it, I don't care that you can hear it on Christian radio stations every day of the week, it's still not true. Eternal security is a weak, watered down, totally inadequate, and ultimately unbiblical distortion of the historic evangelical view of the perseverance of the saints. Saints persevere. That's what this verse says. They obtain salvation by means of grace expressing itself in persevering faith. That is in the Bible.

I want to be very clear here because I have been falsely accused from time to time of teaching that people can lose their salvation. If I have ever said that, even accidentally, I apologise and retract. However, that's not what I mean to say and that's not what I believe. *I do not believe that a truly converted person falls away.* What I believe is that most Christians are not truly converted, and that those who aren't will *all* fall away; when persecution comes, when trials and tribulations come, the false fall away.

Eternal security is a relatively new doctrine, and that in itself should be cause for concern. The great reformers did not teach eternal security; they taught the perseverance of the saints. Heresy is defined as a teaching that may be partly or even mostly true but in the final analysis is incomplete, inaccurate, and deficient in terms of faith and salvation. Eternal security suggests that everyone who waves their hand or stands in a service or signs a pledge card is eternally saved, and the merit of their decision can never be taken from them. That is *heresy* in several different ways and it damns men and women to hell. Where does it say in the Bible that we are to tell people that they are *securely saved?* Nowhere! Instead you find the great apostles always warning against falling away.

> *Take care*, brothers and sisters, that none of you may have an evil, unbelieving heart that *turns away from the living God*. But exhort one another every day, as long as it is called 'today', *so that none of you may be hardened* by the deceitfulness of sin. For we have become partners of Christ, *if only we hold our first confidence firm to the end*. (Hebrews 3:12–14)

Where is the warrant in that for telling someone who waved their hand at a campfire that they have eternal security? Eternal security is a recent doctrine; it's a recent replacement in evangelical conversation for the old reformed doctrine of the perseverance of the saints. It is no improvement; it is a horrible regression.

Now, I fear that you will think this some strange obsession of mine. It is not. This is what your grandparents believed. This is what Spurgeon and Lloyd Jones believed, and this is what Calvin taught. Let me provide a rather lengthy quote from Wayne Grudem:

> Here we see why the phrase *eternal security* can be quite misleading. In some evangelical churches, instead of offering the full and balanced presentation of the doctrine of the perseverance of the saints, pastors have sometimes taught *a watered down version*, which in effect tells people that all who have made a profession of faith and been baptized are "eternally secure". The result is that *some people who are not genuinely converted at all* may "come forward" at the end of an evangelistic sermon to profess faith in Christ, and may be baptized shortly

after that, but then leave the fellowship of the church and live a life no different from the one they lived before they gained this "eternal security". In this way *people are given false assurance* and are being *cruelly deceived* into *thinking they are going to heaven when in fact they are not.*[6]

The old doctrine of the perseverance of the saints is two-sided. It says that all saints persevere and the saints are those who persevere. Those two sides are equally true or neither is true. What is a Christian but one who has finally, by God's grace, *overcome the world?* If the Gospel is not that, then it is of no value. Eternal security to many today means that if you ever wave your hand at Jesus, you can be assured that you are saved and you can go on living however you choose; you can be a backsliding Christian, always falling away and coming back to embrace the ever-present grace of God. Blasphemy, mockery, and heresy.

Listen to me, friends: many "Christians" will fall away. The truly converted, truly saved, elect church of God will persevere and emerge from her covering of chaff and tare into glorious brilliance through *tribulation, trial, and fiery persection*—this is the will of the Lord and it is glorious when it is properly understood and taught. Blessed are those who are persecuted for righteousness' sake, for theirs is the kingdom of heaven.

If persevering under persecution is so important, how can we partner with that? How can we get better at persevering, especially under persecution? Let me be very clear: it is the grace of God that saves us and the grace of God which *seals* us and effects our perseverance under trial. God does it! God is the first, primary, and irresistible *force* of our preservation. We can no more preserve our faith than we could have given birth to it. And yet the Scripture manages

---

6 Grudem, Wayne. *Systematic Theologiy* (Grand Rapids, MI: Zondervan, 1994), p. 806. Emphasis mine.

to speak about the primary sovereignty of God *and* the cooperation of morally responsible agents in a way we have been struggling to precisely define for two thousand years.

God has *elected* us from before the foundation of the world, and yet it is also true that anyone may come. These are complicated matters and I don't know that any human mind has ever fully grasped them. I don't fully understand how bees fly or, for that matter, how my lights turn on, but I trust that they do and I hope one day to understand those things more fully. I am not stupid or arrogant enough to say that if I can't define it precisely right now, it cannot exist in the universe, and I hope you aren't that arrogant, either. We partner with a sovereign, providential God in persevering.

While our role is far lesser than God's, it is given plenty of mention in Scripture, so we will say a few things about it here. Let me suggest three ways we can partner with God to ensure our perseverance even under fiery trial as Christians:

1. Press into the Word.

In Hebrews 6, the passage about falling away we read above, the argument is set in the context of a running rebuke against the Hebrews for not pressing forward into Scripture. The author had said earlier:

> About this we have much to say that is hard to explain, since you have become dull in understanding. For though by this time you ought to be teachers, you need someone to teach you again the basic elements of the oracles of God. You need milk, not solid food; for everyone who lives on milk, being still an infant, is unskilled in the word of righteousness. But solid food is for the mature, for

those whose faculties have been trained by practice to distinguish good from evil. Therefore let us go on towards perfection, leaving behind the basic teaching about Christ, and not laying again the foundation: repentance from dead works and faith towards God, instruction about baptisms, laying on of hands, resurrection of the dead, and eternal judgement. And we will do this, if God permits. (Hebrews 5:11–6:3)

People who want to sit still under the basic teachings and hear the same introductory messages again and again, week after week, are those most in danger of falling away under trial. If you want to confirm your election and persevere in faith, press forward into the Word of God. Demand Biblical teaching and kick out of your pulpits any preacher who would truncate the Gospel, dumb it down, or make it seeker-friendly.

2. Put feet to your faith.

Don't just read the Scriptures, put them into practice.

But be doers of the word, and not merely hearers who deceive themselves. (James 1:22)

So many "Christians" love to go to small groups and chitchat about this or that. They love to sit under teaching, but they refuse to actually put what they've heard into practice. They are deceiving themselves and will not persevere. The real believer puts foot to faith and God withdraws his grace from those who never do.

3. Think about the future.

Part of our problem in the church today is the fact that we've grown gun-shy when it comes to talking about the future. We've all seen the billboards and the painted vans with the silly predictions and we would just rather keep silent on the whole matter. But that tends to leave our Gospel presentation a little short on the Good News part.

I mean, think about it: in our current presentation, what do we honestly tell people will likely follow their conversion? Do we say that after their conversion life will be easy and trouble-free? No. We tell them that things will get worse. Satan will take an interest in you, the world will hate you, and God will refine you through suffering and persecution. How is that good news? Even the call of the Gospel doesn't really sound like good news, does it? How does Jesus call people into the kingdom? Does he say, "Come and eat ice cream?" Does he say, "Believe in me and I will take your troubles away?" Those sound like good news callings; but is that how Jesus calls us? No, he says:

> Then Jesus told his disciples, "If any want to become my followers, let them deny themselves and take up their cross and follow me. For those who want to save their life will lose it, and those who lose their life for my sake will find it." (Matthew 16:24–25)

Deny myself. Carry my cross and die on it. This is Good News? You'll have to work that out for me. But maybe, some suggest, there is a way of following Jesus that will bypass suffering; Christians in North America have been looking for that way for sixty years now.

Maybe they've found it. Maybe there's a way for a sweet glide into glory? If so, why did Jesus say:

> A disciple is not above the teacher, nor a slave above the master; *it is enough for the disciple to be like the teacher,* and the slave like the master. If they have called the master of the house Beelzebul, how much more will they malign those of his household! Whom to Fear
>
> So have no fear of them; for nothing is covered up that will not be uncovered, and nothing secret that will not become known… Do not fear those who kill the body but cannot kill the soul; rather fear him who can destroy both soul and body in hell. (Matthew 10:24–28, emphasis mine)

So, Jesus has been telling his followers that they will be hated, kicked out of their families, thrown into jail, and tortured and killed if they follow him. Then he says: "Don't think you can do this better than me. That's arrogance! Your goal should be to do this *exactly like me.* Make it your goal to be hated and slandered by the world and to be killed. Don't fear death. People will hate you and kill you, *but the good news* is that they can't throw you into hell." That's the good news? The good news is that if I follow Jesus, everyone will hate me, I will go to jail, and I'll be tortured and killed, *but* I won't go to hell. Yahoo!

But is that the end of the story? No. The really good news comes after the suffering and the being hated and the being kicked out of your family and the being tortured and killed part. We don't talk about that part very much, so the good news sounds like *horrifically bad news* and we wonder why there's so little joy in the church. There is a whole section of *really good news* in our story, but we almost never talk about it because it's the place where silly and contentious people make their beds.

The good news in our Gospel is found in a part of our story called eschatology, which is a fancy word for "last and final things." Eschatology is where the silly people live. This is where the coloured charts are buried. This is where the nasty emails come from, so pastors avoid talking about this topic like the plague. I'm not lying or exaggerating this; it's real and it's a brilliant ploy of the devil.

To make the good news sound like bad news, all you have to do is cut out the last chapter of our story. How do you do that? Get ignorant, divisive, silly people to make it their specialty. Pastors hate conflict and prefer nice emails, so they don't preach on these topics. I got an email a while back because I made a comment about the Rapture not being explicitly taught in Scripture, so this fellow felt the need to chastise me that, as a result of not preaching the pre-tribulational rapture, will be left behind when it happens. I will not be raptured and will be counted among the heathens. Really? Because I preach the mainstream viewpoint that has been the majority position in Evangelical Protestantism since the Reformation? Because of that, I'm going to be left behind? Because I preach what Martin Luther preached, what John Calvin preached, what Jonathon Edwards preached, what Spurgeon preached, what Leon Morris and F.F. Bruce preach, I'm not saved? I find that hard to believe.

So, let me tell you what I've decided. I'm going to tell you people the whole good news and I'm not going to be deterred by the coloured chartists and the emailers. I won't let the devil change our story and I recommend that you not let him shorten yours. Read Revelation, read Matthew 24–25, read 1 Corinthians 15, read Ezekiel 40–48, and read Isaiah 65. Learn those things, believe those promises, and you will be able to rejoice when you suffer for Christ. You will be assured that those promises are your possession. Rejoice and be exceedingly glad, for great is your reward *in heaven*.

The Kingdom of Heaven … and Great Reward

As we've mentioned several times, with most eschatological promises there is a sense in which the thing promised will be realized in an ultimate sense after the Second Coming and the Renewal of all things. Simultaneously, there's a sense in which we have the first fruits, the down payment, the initial experience of the thing promised in the here and now.

So here. Here we are promised that those who prove their faith through suffering can be assured their part in the kingdom of heaven. With the additional detail that this particular beatitude affords us, we can expand on that and say that they shall receive the kingdom of heaven and in it *great reward*. Given the general pattern of these promises, we expect to see some signs of possession and reward in the immediate experience of such folks. Then, ultimately, we expect to see the full measure in the age to come.

Let's begin by discussing the first fruits, or deposit, of this promise. What signs and deposits of the kingdom of heaven and what reward do we see in the present experience of those who are persecuted for righteousness' sake? Peter spoke of this in 1 Peter 4:

> If you are insulted for the name of Christ, you are blessed, *because the Spirit of glory and of God rests upon you.* (1 Peter 4:14, ESV, emphasis mine)

There is a particular promise of power and presence that is the immediate possession of people suffering persecution for the cause of the Gospel and the name of Christ. Scripture speaks of this often:

When they deliver you over, do not be anxious how you are to speak or what you are to say, for what you are to say will be given to you in that hour. For it is not you who speak, but the Spirit of your Father speaking through you. Brother will deliver brother over to death, and the father his child, and children will rise against parents and have them put to death, and you will be hated by all for my name's sake. But the one who endures to the end will be saved. When they persecute you in one town, flee to the next, for truly, I say to you, you will not have gone through all the towns of Israel before the Son of Man comes. A disciple is not above his teacher, nor a servant above his master. It is enough for the disciple to be like his teacher, and the servant like his master. If they have called the master of the house Beelzebul, how much more will they malign those of his household. So have no fear of them, for nothing is covered that will not be revealed, or hidden that will not be known. What I tell you in the dark, say in the light, and what you hear whispered, proclaim on the housetops. And do not fear those who kill the body but cannot kill the soul. Rather fear him who can destroy both soul and body in hell. Are not two sparrows sold for a penny? And not one of them will fall to the ground apart from your Father. But even the hairs of your head are all numbered. Fear not, therefore; you are of more value than many sparrows. So everyone who acknowledges me before men, I also will acknowledge before my Father who is in heaven, but whoever denies me before men, I also will deny before my Father who is in heaven. (Matthew 10:19–33, ESV, emphasis mine)

All three of the synoptic Gospels (Matthew, Mark, and Luke) record this promise. Read it carefully. It promises two great blessings to those who are being persecuted for Jesus' sake. First of all, it promises a heavy anointing from the Holy Spirit over your testimony and defence. This is not a promise to be claimed by lazy pastors who don't wish to spend time in their studies to prepare for the Sunday sermon. Those pastors need to listen to Paul's command to Timothy where he says:

> Study to show thyself approved unto God, a workman that needeth not to be ashamed, rightly dividing the word of truth. (2 Timothy 2:15, KJV)

No, this promise is not an excuse not to study; it's a promise that when you preach under persecution, you preach with the *power of God* resting on you. You preach like you've got one foot in heaven already! That's a great promise. It also promises assurance of salvation. Peter read his sufferings as proof of his salvation and he rejoiced in that, wondered over that, and marvelled that he was accounted worthy. Jesus said very clearly in this passage:

> So *everyone who acknowledges me before men, I also will acknowledge before my Father who is in heaven,* but whoever denies me before men, I also will deny before my Father who is in heaven. (Matthew 10:32–33, ESV, emphasis mine)

Do you want to know for sure you are saved? Preach the Gospel with your head in the noose. Preach the Gospel from between prison bars. Acknowledge Christ as Lord and Saviour before those who hold power over your life and freedom. Do that and you need not doubt. My friends, we offer assurance of salvation way too cheaply in the church today. To every teary-eyed teenager who lifts his hand at a campfire we promise that he will see Jesus when he dies, never mind the fact that we said nothing about sin and repentance, never mind that we told him nothing about humility or Lordship, never mind that he thinks he has signed up for the short-bus to glory… *never mind!* We are so unthinking in the way we present the Gospel today and so hasty in our offer of assurance.

Before we even know if a person is truly converted, we make promises we are ill-positioned to make. The puritans knew better. The puritans said that assurance of salvation was something possessed only after a lifetime of perseverance, obedience, and suffering. That sounds more like what the Bible says. Peter rejoiced *after he persevered under trial!* His perseverance proved to him that Jesus had changed his heart. He remembered how quickly he had wilted under pressure before, but now it was clear to all, it was clear to *Peter,* that he was a changed man! Peter knew that everything was different now, that the grace of God had *changed him* because now he was a *rock* upon which the anger of men was welcome to hurl and cast itself for he would *not move*. Persecution brings us more fully under the anointing of the Holy Spirit and more deeply into the assurance of our salvation. Blessed are those who are persecuted for righteousness' sake, for theirs is the kingdom of heaven—right here, right now on planet earth.

Of course, we look beyond even these wonderful first fruits to the rewards and blessings that lie ahead. There is nothing wrong with that. Indeed, we are commanded to be future thinking, Jesus says:

> Do not lay up for yourselves treasures on earth, where moth and rust destroy and where thieves break in and steal, but lay up for yourselves treasures in heaven, where neither moth nor rust destroys and where thieves do not break in and steal. (Matthew 6:19–20, ESV)

Jesus tells us to store up treasure in heaven and he tells us how to do it:

> Then Peter said in reply, "See, we have left everything and followed you. What then will we have?"
> Jesus said to them, "Truly, I say to you, in the new world, when the Son of Man will sit on his glorious throne, you who have followed me will also sit on twelve thrones, judging the twelve tribes of Israel. And everyone who has left houses or brothers or sisters or father or mother or children or lands, for my name's sake, will receive a hundredfold and will inherit eternal life." (Matthew 19:27–29, ESV)

Jesus didn't rebuke Peter for planning on future reward. Instead he told him how to maximize his portfolio! When you read the Book of Revelation, you cannot help but notice the curious way that the elect people of God are described as they stand in heaven:

> I saw under the altar the souls of *those who had been slain for the word of God and for the witness they had borne.* They cried out with a loud voice, "O Sovereign Lord, holy and true, how long before you will judge and avenge our blood on those who

dwell on the earth?" Then they were each given a white robe and told to rest a little longer, until the number of their fellow servants and their brothers should be complete, *who were to be killed as they themselves had been.* (Revelation 6:9–11, ESV, emphasis mine)

Here John sees that all the people who die in the Lord before his Return are gathered as souls under the altar of God. He sees them being comforted and clothed and told to wait a little longer, but what's really interesting is how they are described. They are called *"those who had been slain for the word of God and for the witness they had borne."* They are those who had been persecuted for righteousness' sake. Truly theirs is the kingdom of heaven. They wait for the rest of the elect people of God who will be *killed, as they had been.* The kingdom of heaven is the exclusive possession of those who are persecuted for righteousness' sake. No other people are there.

Look at Revelation 20, a passage we studied earlier:

> Then I saw thrones, and seated on them were those to whom the authority to judge was committed. Also I saw the souls of those who had been beheaded for the testimony of Jesus and for the word of God, and who had not worshiped the beast or its image and had not received its mark on their foreheads or their hands. They came to life and reigned with Christ for a thousand years. (Revelation 20:4, ESV)

Of course, this is symbolic language. It would be ridiculous to think that the only people who get to reign with Jesus in the age to come are those who were beheaded. What about Peter? He was only crucified. What about John? He was only left to rot in prison. What about Barnabas? He was only burned with fire. No, we mustn't be quite that literal. This is simply a symbolic way of saying, *"Blessed are those who are persecuted for righteousness' sake, for theirs is the kingdom of heaven."*

Are their greater and lesser rewards given for those who have been more fruitful and less fruitful? Who have endured greater and lesser persecutions? Yes, but that hardly seems to matter a great deal. The bottom line is, heaven is the possession of the martyrs—those whose witness went forth in blood, those who were rejected by the same world that rejected their Master. They get heaven. Everything else is secondary. They see Jesus. They serve before the throne and behold the *face of God*. It is enough. It is everything. It is *the reward*.

> Blessed are you when they revile and persecute you, and say all kinds of evil against you falsely for My sake. Rejoice and be exceedingly glad, for great is your reward in heaven, for so they persecuted the prophets who were before you. (Matthew 5:11–12, NKJV)

Small Group Discussion

The eighth beatitude says, *"Blessed are those who are persecuted for righteousness' sake, for theirs is the kingdom of heaven."* As always, the issue of ethics (how we should live and behave) is connected to eschatology (some promise or description of ultimate end-time reality). This glorious promise—and indeed, this present provision—should equip and inspire us to persevere under persecution, and even to rejoice within it. Let's read the texts below to continue that conversation and then, having read the texts, take some time to address the comprehension task that follows.

Matthew 5:10–12
Luke 6:26
2 Corinthians 4:16–18
2 Corinthians 6:1–10
1 Peter 2:13–17
1 Peter 3:13–22
1 Peter 4:1–6
1 Peter 4:12–19
Revelation 6:9–11

Take a moment and consider the fourteen statements below. Circle all that you think correctly reflect what the Bible says about being persecuted for righteousness' sake.

1. If a person has never been physically beaten, imprisoned, or executed, they cannot be considered a truly converted person.
2. If a person is well thought of by all and refuses to take a stand for unpopular truths, they cannot be understood as properly converted.
3. The mark of a successful minister of the Gospel is popularity, prosperity, good health, and success.
4. If a person loves the world too much, it can shipwreck his faith and hamper their ministry.
5. The government will always be against us as Christians. Therefore, we are against the government.

6. Christians who break the law should be prepared to pay the assigned penalty regardless of whether they broke the law for their conscience's sake or not.
7. A Christian who has suffered persecution and persevered is unlikely to ever sin again.
8. Any Christian who expects to be only healthy, happy, and prosperous is eventually going to face a severely destabilizing event when suffering finally comes.
9. The more you are pressed and persecuted, the more provision from the Holy Spirit you are likely to enjoy. Therefore, you cannot look into your heart in times of peace and prosperity and truly know how you will fare under trial. God gives you the grace when you need it.
10. If a Christian denied Christ to avoid torture, he would be revealed as unconverted and destined for hell.
11. It is wrong for a Christian to seek out persecution so as to increase eternal reward. We should simply serve faithfully and courageously, whether we live in a time of hostile or relatively passive social resistance.
12. When the Gospel is generally accepted within a host culture, it's likely proof that the Gospel has been perverted, tamed, and ruined.
13. If you are generally respected as a good person, that probably means you are not a Christian.
14. Simply living the Christian life with integrity and visibility tends to make people feel judged. Whatever you don't do that they do feels like a condemnation to them. Even if they respect you, they will resent you and may speak evil against you.

Personal Reflection and Evaluation

The Bible says:

> But be doers of the word, and not merely hearers who deceive themselves. For if any are hearers of the word and not doers, they are like those who look at themselves in a mirror; for they look at themselves and, on going away, immediately forget what they were like. But those who look into the perfect law, the law of liberty, and persevere, being not hearers who forget but doers who act— *they will be blessed in their doing.* (James 1:22–25, emphasis mine)

The beatitudes are a description of what *every* Christian should look like. We would be the greatest of fools not to ask a simple follow up question: "To what extent do I look this way? Am I persecuted and reviled for righteousness' sake?"

Take some time and carefully consider the following ten statements. If the statement is *always true of you,* give yourself a score of ten. If it is *sometimes true of you,* give yourself a five. If it is *rarely or never true of you,* give yourself a zero. Tally your score out of a hundred when you have completed the exercise.

1. I have suffered financially because of my steadfast commitment to Jesus Christ.
2. I have suffered slander because of my steadfast commitment to Jesus Christ.
3. I have experienced the rejection or reviling of my family members because of my steadfast commitment to Jesus Christ.

4. I have missed out on opportunities to save money, make money, or get a promotion because of my commitment to the ethical teaching of Jesus Christ.
5. I have felt belittled or marginalised because of my beliefs as a Christian.
6. I have had people refer to me as "old-fashioned," "sexist," "traditional," "mean," or "unloving" because of my beliefs as a Christian and my practices as a follower of Jesus Christ.
7. I have experienced physical difficulties and abuse because of my steadfast faith in Jesus Christ and my proclamation of the Gospel.
8. I have come afoul of the government because of my Gospel beliefs and activities.
9. I have experienced the special empowerment of the Holy Spirit to speak boldly when under duress or when the name of Christ is being maligned.
10. I have experienced the assuring testimony of the Holy Spirit within my soul when I have withstood persecution by the grace of God.

My score out of 100: _____

Evaluated on this date: _____

My prayer of honest response to the Lord:

Chapter Nine

The Witnesss of the Fully Converted Church—Salt and Light

Jesus has no doubt that the Christian life will be undeniably distinctive and compelling. He describes the fully converted life and then declares:

> You are the salt of the earth, but if salt has lost its taste, how shall its saltiness be restored? It is no longer good for anything except to be thrown out and trampled under people's feet. You are the light of the world. A city set on a hill cannot be hidden. Nor do people light a lamp and put it under a basket, but on a stand, and it gives light to all in the house. In the same way, let your light shine before others, so that they may see your good works and give glory to your Father who is in heaven. (Matthew 5:13–16, ESV)

If people live a fully converted life inside a dark and dying world, they will begin to participate in an unavoidable and automatic dynamic. We don't do faith in a vacuum; we live in a world filled with people who will react to how we live. Jesus now begins to unpack this dynamic. He says firstly that if we live a fully converted life, we will be the salt of the earth.

The Salt of the Earth

Salt in those days was used for two things: flavour and preservation. Salt tastes different and better than the stuff you put it on and it also keeps those things from rotting. That's a pretty powerful metaphor. Jesus is saying that if we really live this way, if by God's grace and through his Holy Spirit we actually live fully converted lives and if we do it together as a Body, we will build an alternative community that tastes and smells better than the dying, putrefying world that everyone else is living in. They'll want to be a part of it and, even if they reject it, the mere presence of it will bless the world and slow its rate of death.

But there is a fairly huge caveat thrown in there, which I'm sure you noticed:

> …but if salt has lost its taste, how shall its saltiness be restored? It is no longer good for anything except to be thrown out and trampled under people's feet. (Matthew 5:13, ESV)

If the church becomes no different than the world, it is no longer good for anything and is exposed to trampling and is subject to rejection. In those days, salt might lose its astringency (meaning zestiness and distinctive, sharp flavour) by becoming mixed with sand. Imagine that you filled a saltshaker half with salt and half with sand and then sprinkled that on your French fries. What would you do? You would spit those fries onto the table, rinse out your mouth with water, then dump the shaker into the garbage. It is *too mixed* to be of any value. This is a clear warning against mixture and compromise. We find Jesus using different imagery, but saying the exact same thing in the Book of Revelation:

> I know your works; you are neither cold nor hot. I wish that you were either cold or hot. So, because you are lukewarm, and neither cold nor hot, I am about to spit you out of my mouth. (Revelation 3:15–16)

Hot water is good for washing or bathing and cold water is good for drinking, but when they are mixed together you get lukewarm water, which is good for nothing and is spat out onto the floor. Some things *should not be mixed!* Jesus has just finished preaching on the high cost of discipleship, the high call of the fully converted life, and here in the very next verse Jesus warns us that if we fail to take this teaching seriously, we will fill the church with sand and lose all of our savour and distinctiveness… and we won't get it back. We will be mixed, useless, tasteless, and ruined.

Fully converted lives produce an attractive, alternative community that draws people in. They see the humility, they see the love and care, they see the integrity and the mercy, and they say, "I want in!" Or alternatively, they may say, "I feel judged!" A fully converted community works like a wedge into its host and forces people to divide—just like Jesus said in Matthew 10:

> Do not think that I have come to bring peace to the earth. I have not come to bring peace, but a sword.

> For I have come to set a man against his father, and a daughter against her mother, and a daughter-in-law against her mother-in-law. And a person's enemies will be those of his own household. (Matthew 10:34–36, ESV)

People saw Jesus and the life he lived and some of them said, "Surely this man is the Son of God!" Others said, "He has a demon." Nobody said, "What's for dinner?" A truly converted life, smelling of heaven in the midst of a dead and rotting world, will cause a reaction! You cannot ignore it. It is the smell of life when all around is death.

Did you know that the term "Gospel" is actually a kind of sensual word? The etymology of the word comes from Roman times. It was originally used to describe how victories were announced to the populace. There would be particular incense burnings associated with the proclamation, helping to generate enthusiasm for the victory. Gospel means "Good News" and it references how that Good News is spread. You can hear hints of that in 2 Corinthians 2:

> But thanks be to God, who in Christ always leads us in triumphal procession, and through us spreads the fragrance of the knowledge of him everywhere. For we are the aroma of Christ to God among those who are being saved and among those who are perishing, to one a fragrance from death to death, to the other a fragrance from life to life. (2 Corinthians 2:14–16, ESV)

The Apostle Paul is saying that fully converted Christians—*real believers*—are like the smell of victory in a dying world! The very smell of them is a message that someone has triumphed and that person is Jesus Christ. No one could live this way unless someone had defeated sin and death and sowed seeds of life and victory among the crowd! The Gospel message and the converted church is thus a fragrance of life to some—some people will smell it, sense its differentness, be attracted, and move forward into life through Christ—while others will smell only death—the death of their godhood, the death of their lusts, the death of their arrogance—and turn away, feeling judged and assaulted. We don't control these things, but we instigate them automatically by the nature of our converted living.

You are the salt of the earth.

The Light of the World

Jesus says also:

> You are the light of the world. A city set on a hill cannot be hidden. Nor do people light a lamp and put it under a basket, but on a stand, and it gives light to all in the house. In the same way, let your light shine before others, so that they may see your good works and give glory to your Father who is in heaven. (Matthew 5:14–16, ESV)

Light is sometimes a symbol of truth in the Bible, but most scholars interpret this as a parallel metaphor to salt, meaning that it, too, is intended as a description of differentness. Jesus is further developing how this dynamic of differentness will play out in witness. He says that we are like a city on a hill that cannot be hidden. That would have made a lot more sense to first-century readers than it does to us. We live in a well-lit world. There are very few places you can go and experience total darkness.

When I was a youth pastor, I used to lead canoe trips in the backcountry of Algonquin Provincial Park. I recall one trip, which we had rather foolishly labelled "The Man Mountain Experience." We intended to cover well over sixty miles in five days, and unfortunately we had to do most of that in very bad weather. It rained most days and was overcast most nights. When you're in the Canadian backcountry late at night with an overcast sky, you will experience total darkness. You can put your hand five inches in front of your face and still not see it. That was the way it was all the time in the ancient world—unless you lived near a city.

When I was a boy, I lived in a small green belt between a big city and small city. The small city was over a hill and far away but the big city was sixty kilometers south across mostly flat land. The area where I lived had excellent soil for farming and so had been wisely zoned as a development-free region. We lived in a small subdivision in the middle of a giant patch of farmers' fields! At night, when it was overcast, the sky above was dark and foreboding, but if you looked downward towards the big city in the south there was a constant orange glow. It was like a nightlight in the hallway of a dark house. It was just enough to take the fear out of night.

Jesus says that the church—the community of the fully converted—will function just that way. To those living in outer darkness it will look different, alive, and close and it will give hope to those who are lost and scared. Jesus says that we are the light of the world, that we are a city on a hill that cannot be hid. But then he adds a caveat:

> Nor do people light a lamp and put it under a basket, but on a stand, and it gives light to all in the house. (Matthew 5:15, ESV)

We cannot hide who we are. This is an important teaching to people who've just been told that if they live the fully converted Christian life, they will arouse the hostility of many in the world and face revilement and persecution. One might hear that and say in one's heart, "Then I must live the fully converted life in shadow! I must live away from the world so that my differentness does not offend and incite persecution." But that would leave the world without hope. That would leave the lost in the dark and in fear. The fully converted life must be different, but it must also be near. Not near in terms of compromise, not near in terms of likeness to the lostness of the world, but rather near in terms of visibility and accessibility. We must live differently, visibly, publicly, and accessibly if we want to be the light of the world.

The nature of this light is not left to our imagination. Jesus tells us what the metaphor of light stands for. He says:

> In the same way, let your light shine before others, so that *they may see your good works* and give glory to your Father who is in heaven. (Matthew 5:16, ESV, emphasis mine)

In this metaphor, our light is not our sound theology, though that is very important. Neither is it our Gospel preaching, though that is also very important. Our light is our collective good deeds. People should look at how we serve one another and say, "See how they love each other! See how they honour the aged! See how they care for their widows! See how they raise their children! See how they raise the fatherless and the orphan in their midst!" Jesus said that our love for one another would be our identifying witness:

> By this all people will know that you are my disciples, if you have love for one another. (John 13:35. ESV)

Too often in Christendom I hear people talk as though the only fit object for the charitable impulse is the care of the unsaved. Everyone will pat you on the back if you dig a well for a Muslim village in northern Nigeria. Everyone will sing your praises if you spoon out soup to foul-mouthed addicts in the big city. But people will accuse you of being selfish and insular when you try calling people to love one another within the church. But the Apostle Paul was so clear on this:

> And let us not grow weary of doing good, for in due season we will reap, if we do not give up. So then, as we have opportunity, let us do good to everyone, and especially to those who are of the household of faith. (Galatians 6:9–10, ESV)

Why especially the household of faith? Because if we don't do a fantastic job of loving one another, if we don't serve each other and care for one another in the church, no one will come near enough to hear the Gospel! We will be the salt that has lost its saltiness, the light under a bushel, the church that looks no better than the world. Listen to me, friend: I know that the story of the Good Samaritan is in the Bible. It's in my version, too, and I believe that teaching. I believe that as a fully converted Christian, it is my responsibility to show mercy on whomever the Lord puts in my path. I must love and serve my neighbour, who is defined by Jesus as "the needy person on my path." I believe that with all my heart. But I also believe that whatever we are prepared to do for that needy person on the path, we need to do one more for the needy brother or sister in our midst. Love the neighbour, yes! Love the sister, love the brother all the more. We have to build a better city, my friends! We have to build a converted community full of people who live and love like Jesus. That is the hope of the world. That's what will call them out of darkness and into his marvellous light. God will do it. God is doing it, and he is doing it through His Body, the church.

I want to say this next part very carefully. Many of my friends and brothers in Christ use this language, and I love them very much, but I wish it would stop. Many people, good people, talk about how Christians need to be less religious and more relational. I know what they mean by that, I really do. I know that they mean we should not be hypocrites and legalists and that we should love God and love our neighbour and stick to the basics. I totally agree with that. The problem is that the Bible describes religion in very similar terms. The Bible says:

> Religion that is pure and undefiled before God, the Father, is this: to care for orphans and widows in their distress, and to keep oneself unstained by the world. (James 1:27)

The Bible says that there is a good way to be religious. It involves building a community around two principles: converted character and loving service. I long for that kind of religion! I want more of that, not less of that! I believe that if we built churches like this, full of fully converted people living lives of character and loving service, we wouldn't need conferences on evangelism and books on how to be contagious; we would instead need books and conferences on discipleship and integration and volunteer training, because we wouldn't be able to keep people from converting!

I'm not saying that a fully converted community makes preaching the Gospel of God unnecessary. I've never liked that quote from St. Francis about preaching the Gospel at all times, with words if necessary—I don't think that's true. The Gospel is a Word and it must be spoken. The Bible is clear about that.

> But how are they to call on him in whom they have not believed? And how are they to believe in him of whom they have never heard? And how are they to hear without someone preaching? (Romans 10:14, ESV)

I want every Christian to be a Gospel preacher. I just think it would be a lot more effective if people could smell us and see us from miles away. I think it would be more effective and more fruitful if they already knew by the manner of our life and living that a victory had been won somewhere by someone who promised hope. I think our preaching would bring in a bigger harvest if the church lived as salt and light.

There is a fabulous little book I love called *The Rise of Christianity* by Rodney Stark. Rodney Stark isn't a Christian author per se; he's a sociologist. He wrote this book not to promote Christian virtue but rather to answer a question that has puzzled historians for almost two thousand years. How did a small Jewish sect numbering no more than three to five thousand people by the year A.D. 60 become the majority religion in the Roman Empire by the year 300? Think about that for a moment. In the time of the Apostle Paul, there were just over three to five thousand Christians, the historians estimate. None of the churches he wrote to had more than a hundred people in them, except perhaps the church in Rome. Two hundred fifty years later, there are at least thirty million Christians. How did that happen? Even scholars who don't love Jesus wrestle with this as one of the most amazing miracles in history. Do you know what the near consensus answer is? Now, remember that these people don't believe in the Holy Spirit or God's sovereignty over history, so you and I might add a few key details, but their observation is still worth looking at. The reason for this growth, according to historians, is the ethic of humble service within the early Christian community.

Christians were famous for providing basic nursing to their own sick and elderly, something pagans didn't do. Most Roman pagans had no concept of life after death, so they rarely would have contact with sick people, fearing to catch whatever they had. They left their old and infirm to die in isolation. The Christians not only cared for their own poor, but would also go into the homes of the sick and dying pagans and nurse them.

There were two great plagues in the Roman Empire that decimated the population. The first occurred during the reign of Marcus Aurelius, made famous to modern people through the movie *Gladiator*. Unlike in the movie, in actual history Aurelius died in the plague. During that plague, thirty percent of the pagan population died. The Christian death rate was less than ten percent. Why? Well, you and I might talk about the Holy Spirit and quote Psalm 91, but the historians will tell you it was because basic nursing cuts down mortality rates by two-thirds. There was another plague fifty years after that, and again thirty percent of the pagan population perished and again good Christian men and women, with no thought of their own lives, changed the sheets, emptied the chamber pots, and spooned broth to their sick pagan neighbours and yet their mortality rate was less than ten percent.

This became pretty convincing evidence of the superiority of our God and faith, resulting in a massive conversion of pagans to Christianity. Pagans wanted to be part of a society where the rich cared for the poor and where the healthy nursed the sick. They wanted to worship a God who had power over disease and whose servants acted like they believed it. By the time they came near enough to hear the preaching, they were already convinced that the Christian God was victorious over death and darkness. The church was different. The church was the aroma of victory. The church was a city on a hill and people came out of the darkness and found the light.

Let me be clear: this is not a call for the social Gospel or for integral mission. This is just a call for fully converted Christians to live visibly, publically, and accessibly so that they could use what God had done in them as a catalyst for Gospel preaching! Don't mix, don't hide, and don't cover. Be the church! Be the salt of the earth, be the light of the world, be the hope of the nations! Let the mountain of the Lord's house be lifted up higher than every other mountain and let the nations stream to it! If you do that:

> Many peoples shall come, and say: "Come, let us go up to the mountain of the Lord, to the house of the God of Jacob, that he may teach us his ways and that we may walk in his paths." For out of Zion shall go the law, and the word of the Lord from Jerusalem. He shall judge between the nations, and shall decide disputes for many peoples; and they shall beat their swords into plowshares, and their spears into pruning hooks; nation shall not lift up sword against nation, neither shall they learn war anymore. *O house of Jacob, come, let us walk in the light of the Lord.* (Isaiah 2:3–5, ESV, emphasis mine)

Even so, come Lord Jesus.

As mentioned back in Chapter One, we made the decision not to include all of the Frequently Asked Questions (FAQ) in the published text of this book, as we had done with *Mile 1*. You can see the questions and the answers we have provided to users by visiting: www.beaconcitypublishing.com.

I highly recommend visiting the site to engage with the questions, particularly those related to this last chapter. When we're talking about the witness of the church and preserving our distinctiveness, we are led inevitably into a discussion about church discipline and judgment. Failure to wrestle with those questions can rob you of effectiveness and ministry, imperiling the very souls of the lost people we live among.

If you're leading small groups around this material, don't assume you can answer questions out of your experience or instinctive convictions. It has been so long since we've thought straight and taught straight on this that you may need a quick refresher. That's what the site is for.

We who walk the narrow way walk in the footsteps of great men and women who have gone before. We need to be humble enough to learn from them. We are not the first to go this way. By God's grace, we will not be the last. Let's talk to each other and bless each other along the way.

Small Group Discussion

Jesus calls on us to be salt and light. The distinctive and compelling life of the fully converted church must be part and parcel of our witness to the world. Let's read the texts below to continue that conversation and then, having read the texts, take some time to address the comprehension task that follows.

> Matthew 5:13–16
> Luke 14:34–35
> James 2:14–26
> John 13:31–35
> Galatians 6:9–10
> Acts 2:40–47
> Acts 4:32–37
> Acts 5:1–16
> Isaiah 2:1–22

Take a moment and consider the fourteen statements below. Circle all that you think correctly reflect what the Bible says about us being salt and light.

1. If being tangibly different from the world we live in is so important, maybe a little less emphasis should be put on making the church "seeker-friendly." Maybe what people are looking for is something totally different than the world they are living in.
2. If being "unmixed" and astringent is so important to the witness of the church, maybe we should spend a little more time making sure people are fully converted before we welcome them into church membership.
3. The early church grew very fast because there were signs and wonders occurring on a more frequent basis.
4. If I don't have the gift of evangelism, there's no way for me to participate in the work of the Gospel. Evangelism is for the talkers and preachers.
5. I can make a strong contribution to the cause of the Gospel by living as a fully converted person, with holiness and mercy within view of my friends and neighbours who are perishing.
6. A church that does a great job of living holy and unstained by the world, while at the same time doing a great job of loving and serving its members and neighbours, should find a very receptive audience for its Gospel preaching.
7. All this teaching simply proves that you don't need preaching to get out the Gospel message. Actions speak louder than words.
8. All Gospel ministry is about going. We come to church to be built up, but we go out to share the Gospel. Church and evangelism are different things. Much Gospel ministry is attractional. People come to the church because it smells

different and it looks hopeful. They then hear the truth preached and are prepared to believe it.
9. It is possible for a church to take holiness seriously and still be attractional. Holiness and converted living are not necessarily unappealing to lost people.
10. If a church doesn't put serious time and resources into the loving care of its membership—particularly the elderly, widows and orphans—no matter how good the preaching is, the lost people won't buy it.
11. If a church is full of truly converted people who live holy and compassionate lives in a visible, accessible way, everyone in town will likely become a Christian.
12. If you want your church to be evangelistically fruitful, it is likely wise to start by seeking the full conversion of your membership and then embarking on a season of intense growth and recommitment to converted character and loving service. If you attempt to be too evangelistic before you are yourself fully converted, you are unlikely to see great results.
13. Given this teaching by Jesus, there's probably no place for monks in monasteries or nuns in convents. Salt in a shaker is of little use. Being holy without contact is wholly useless.

Personal Reflection and Evaluation

The Bible says:

> But be doers of the word, and not merely hearers who deceive themselves. For if any are hearers of

the word and not doers, they are like those who look at themselves in a mirror; for they look at themselves and, on going away, immediately forget what they were like. But those who look into the perfect law, the law of liberty, and persevere, being not hearers who forget but doers who act— *they will be blessed in their doing.* (James 1:22–25, emphasis mine)

The Beatitudes are a description of what *every* Christian should look like and the consequent call to witness is not presented in a way that would suggest it is in any way optional. Because of the more corporate nature of witness, as opposed to the more individual issue of being fully converted, these questions are posed in a collective sense. They encourage you to think about your church and the quality of its saltiness and luminescence. Is your church the salt of the earth? Is it the light of the world? Is it the hope of your city?

Take some time and carefully consider the following ten statements. If the statement is *always true of you,* give yourself a score of ten. If it is *sometimes true of you,* give yourself a five. If it is *rarely or never true of you,* give yourself a zero. Tally your score out of a hundred when you have completed the exercise. My church takes conversion and baptism seriously. They go beyond the hand wave and the leaders actually meet with people to ensure that they understand the Gospel and are truly converted.

14. My church takes membership seriously. There is a much-heightened level of accountability for members.
15. My church takes growth and holiness seriously. There are groups that explain what Christian life looks like and what changes are necessary in order to *convert* to the way of

Christ. They do not stop at the decision. They understand that beyond the decision there is a walk.
16. My church takes church discipline seriously. Even though it is painful and no fun at all, they understand that if sin is left to fester, it harms the person sinning, it harms the church, and it harms the lost people who are now less likely to come and hear the saving Gospel. Ideally they seek restoration, but if a member persists in sin against all counsel, they will remove that person for the sake of the mission and the honour of Christ's name.
17. My church takes member care seriously. They work together to care for seniors, understanding that this cannot be left to the pastor or a paid staffer. This is our job. We bring food and cheer to older folks in need.
18. My church is a father to the fatherless and a husband to the widow. They place a high emphasis on caring for single mothers within the church and for helping them raise up their kids.
19. My church places a high emphasis on caring for the sick. There is visitation and home support offered to members in need.
20. My church extends this loving ministry beyond the membership to needy folks in the community. We care for each other especially, but our loving service tends to overflow and bless those we live among.
21. My church doesn't compromise on holiness or truth issues and yet we still see an awful lot of new people.
22. My church is respected by many in the community but also resented by many. We are not universally loved, but they would sure notice if we disappeared.

My score out of 100: _____

Evaluated on this date: _____

My prayer of honest response to the Lord:

_____

_____

_____

_____

_____

_____

Epilogue

Every generation in Christendom has fought a battle to preserve the Gospel. The direction of the assault is different, century by century, but the aim of the enemy hasn't changed: to deceive if possible, even the elect. The battle in our day is against what was once called "easy believism" or at other times "cheap grace" and is now sometimes referred to as "transactionalism." The devil wants to blur the lines so as to convince as many people as possible that they are Christians when in fact they are not. There is no person so lost as the person convinced they are saved who is, in fact, mistaken. The devil knows his Bible and he recalls that Jesus said:

> On that day many will say to me, "Lord, Lord, did we not prophesy in your name, and cast out demons in your name, and do many mighty works in your name?" And then will I declare to them, "I never knew you; depart from me, you workers of lawlessness." (Matthew 7:22–23, ESV)

The devil just wants to maximize that "many." He wants as many people as possible to put confidence in their sincere profession ("Lord, Lord!"), or their spiritual gifts (which can be faked and counterfeited) or their good works (which can be deceitful). He wants to rob God of glory and rob his children of eternal life.

The devil has managed to convince a lot of "Christians" that they are in, that they are assured, that their tearful prayer many years ago was *magic,* and the sincerity of that moment unassailable. He wants to steal from them the blessings associated by grace with the fully converted life in Christ. The Apostle Paul was concerned about this. He wrote in 1 Corinthians 10:

> I want you to know, brothers, that our fathers were all under the cloud, and all passed through the sea, and all were baptized into Moses in the cloud and in the sea, and all ate the same spiritual food, and all drank the same spiritual drink. For they drank from the spiritual Rock that followed them, and the Rock was Christ. Nevertheless, with most of them God was not pleased, for they were overthrown in the wilderness. Now these things took place as examples for us, that we might not desire evil as they did. Do not be idolaters as some of them were; as it is written, "The people sat down to eat and drink and rose up to play." We must not indulge in sexual immorality as some of them did, and twenty-three thousand fell in a single day. We must not put Christ to the test, as some of them did and were destroyed by serpents, nor grumble, as some of them did and were destroyed by the Destroyer. Now these things happened to them as an example, but they were written down for our instruction, on whom the end of the ages has come.

Epilogue

> Therefore let anyone who thinks that he stands take heed lest he fall. (1 Corinthians 10:1–12, ESV)

Let anyone who thinks he stands take heed lest he fall. He says that it is entirely possible for people who have received spiritual guidance (under the cloud), who have been baptized and received into membership (passed through the sea, baptized into Moses), who have taken communion (ate the spiritual food, drank the spiritual drink) to *die in the desert* because of idolatry. They may love God, but they expect him to share heart space with things of the world and the flesh. They are not fully converted. They have left Egypt, but Egypt still lives in their heart. They die in the desert. *They never cross over into the promises.*

This is in the Bible, my friends! The whole aim of this book has been to help you take heed, lest you fall. I am desperately afraid that the vast majority of North American evangelical Christians are no longer truly saved. Oh, I know they have had spiritual experiences and have felt the promptings of the Holy Spirit and I know they have been baptized and I know they have taken communion and I know that many of them appear to move in gifts and I know that all of that should make me less anxious… but it doesn't.

The church has taken over the devil's game of offering people cheap assurance. We tell them, "If you really meant it, if you felt sincere when you prayed that prayer twenty-eight years ago, it doesn't matter how you live. It doesn't matter that you've been persisting in sin for the last decade. It doesn't matter. You can be assured of your salvation." That's the devil's line. Why does it so often come from our mouths? He wants to put people to sleep so that the first words they hear when they awake are, "I never knew you. Away from me, you evil doer."

I'm not opposed to assurance. I didn't write this book to rob you of your assurance. I wrote this book to draw you back to the only assurance that ever mattered. I want you to read this description of what Jesus said converted life looks like, and then I want you to prayerfully evaluate your life against his divine standard. Then I want you to ask the Holy Spirit, "Has this been born in me?" Let him speak to you. The Bible says:

> The Spirit himself bears witness with our spirit that we are children of God, and if children, then heirs—heirs of God and fellow heirs with Christ, provided we suffer with him in order that we may also be glorified with him. (Romans 8:16–17, ESV)

The Bible says that real assurance of salvation comes from the Holy Spirit bearing witness with our spirit that we are children of God and that this is then confirmed by our persevering in faith under trial and test. That's where the Bible says assurance comes from. You engage with the Spirit—the same Spirit that was in Jesus, the same Spirit by which he ministered and prophesied, the same Spirit by which the Bible was written, by which the beatitudes were given.

Listen to how Jesus, speaking in the Spirit, described fully converted life and then ask the Spirit, "Is this born in me?" If he says yes, and that bears out in your perseverance, then rejoice and be exceedingly glad, for great is your reward in heaven. If he says no, and there is no evidence of that in persevering obedience in test and trial, then go back. Go back to the narrow gate and cry out, "Have mercy on me, a sinner. Grant me the grace to repent as I ought. Cover me with the shed blood of Jesus Christ. All my righteousness is as filthy rags. His blood for my life! Fill me with your Holy Spirit! Take my heart and make it new! Grant me the grace to walk in daily penitence and daily obedience and daily differentness. Make me salt and light for the glory of God and the honour of your name.

Epilogue

Amen." Then stand and in his grace walk the narrow way. God bless you as you go.

To God alone be the glory.